Love Your Life Not Theirs

— 7 MONEY HABITS —
for Living the Life You Want

RACHEL CRUZE

"Godliness with contentment is great gain."
1 TIMOTHY 6:6 NIV

Love Your Life
Not Theirs

—— 7 MONEY HABITS ——
for Living the Life You Want

RACHEL CRUZE

RAMSEY
P R E S S

Published by Ramsey Press, The Lampo Group, LLC
Franklin, Tennessee 37064

This publication is designed to provide accurate and authoritative information with regard to the subject matter covered. It is sold with the understanding that the publisher is not engaged in rendering financial, accounting, or other professional advice. If financial advice or other expert assistance is required, the services of a competent professional should be sought.

Unless otherwise noted, all Scripture quotations are from the Holy Bible, New International Version®, NIV®, Copyright © 1973, 1978, 1984, 2011 by Biblica, Inc.™ Used by permission of Zondervan. All rights reserved worldwide.

Scripture quotations marked ESV are from the ESV® Bible (The Holy Bible, English Standard Version®), copyright © 2001 by Crossway, a publishing ministry of Good News Publishers. Used by permission. All rights reserved.

Editors: Ben Stroup, Allen Harris, Jen Gingerich
Cover Design: Tim Newton
Interior Design: Mandi Cofer

ISBN: 978-1-9370-7797-6

Printed in the United States of America
19 20 21 22 23 WRZ 8 7 6 5 4

— Dedication —

To my daughter, Amelia.

You were with me every step of the way on this book. Finding out I was pregnant with you right as we started working on this project helped me see this book in a new light. Since I started the first drafts while I was pregnant and worked on it throughout your first year, I feel like we wrote this book together. You have brought more joy into my life than I could ever have imagined, and you are by far my greatest accomplishment. I love you more than you'll ever know!

— Acknowledgments —

Turning an idea into a book is one of the hardest, most exciting things I ever get to do! There's no way I'd be able to do it without the help of the amazing team I get to work with every day. I'd like to say a special word of thanks to:

Winston Cruze, for being the most supportive husband in the world. I am so thankful for you cheering me on throughout this process and for believing in me. I fall more in love with you every day!

Dave and Sharon Ramsey, my parents, for giving me the strong foundation that led to the principles in this book. Your strength and courage in facing your past money mistakes have changed our family's future for generations to come.

Allen Harris and Preston Cannon, for your great leadership throughout the editorial and publishing process.

Ben Stroup, my editor for this project, for helping me nail down and organize the million ideas I had for this book.

Jen Gingerich, for your outstanding editorial and developmental help.

Luke LeFevre and Tim Newton, for overseeing all design elements and cover art.

Meg Grunke, my friend and publicist, for helping me get the word out about this book and for sticking with me over thousands of miles and hundreds of media appearances.

Suzanne Simms, Jen Sievertsen, Jeremy Breland, Brian Williams, Blake Thompson, Andy Barton, Cory Mabry, Robert Bruce, Erin McAtee, Lara Johnson, and so many others, for their time, prayers, and hard work as we brought this book to life.

— Contents —

— Foreword —

Dave Ramsey

I've been honored to help people take control of their money for more than twenty-five years. During that time, my team and I have grown a business, Ramsey Solutions, that reaches millions of people every year. And I'd been on the radio, writing books, and building the company for a couple of decades before I had a shocking realization: I'm not going to be around here forever. Genius, right?

One of the fundamental strategic pillars of our organization states, "Our message will be alive and well long after we're gone." Translation: we have more work to do than any of us can do in a lifetime, and our number-one goal for our business is to make sure it continues to make an impact on people's lives for generations to come. That's a big goal, and I knew I needed some big help.

So, several years ago, we started adding new, powerful voices to our team to help carry our message into the next generation. But here's the deal: We had no desire to create bigheaded celebrities and puffed up divas. I have zero patience for speakers who are more concerned about having all the blue M&M's removed from their greenroom than they are about serving the people they're talking to.

We knew from the start that our Ramsey Personalities had to have the confidence and skill to stand in front of tens of thousands of people while having the heart and humility to spend time with the struggling single mom who wants to talk to them after the event. Our personalities had to be completely comfortable in front of a crowd, a microphone, a television camera, and, most importantly, in front of an individual who needed help. I've been around authors and speakers my entire career, and, I promise you, finding that combination of authority and humility is a tough job. But I'm happy to say that we struck gold with the very first personality we added to our team, Rachel Cruze.

In the years Rachel's been on our team, she has held court over huge arena crowds, sharing the stage with some of the most popular, dynamic speakers in the country. She's sat in on my national radio show regularly for years, even hosting the show without me several times like a pro. She's become a number-one best-selling author. She's appeared on some of the highest-rated television morning shows in the country, like *Fox & Friends*, *Good Morning America*, and *TODAY*. She's been a monthly contributor to *Woman's Day* magazine for years. She's featured in America's number-one high school curriculum on personal finance, *Foundations in Personal Finance*. And, inside our walls, Rachel has become a trusted executive and member of our operating board, helping us lead the company into new opportunities and new messages.

Rachel is doing an amazing job spreading the message of hope to an entirely new audience, and I am so excited about the work she's doing! I couldn't ask for more from any speaker, author, or executive on my team. I'm proud to lead her in the work she's doing—but I'm even more proud to be her dad.

Rachel has grown up with these countercultural financial principles her whole life. She knows how to work hard, spend wisely, save diligently, and give generously. She knows how to live a life she loves without the debt, stress, and worry that most people deal with. She knows how to prioritize the things she values. She knows nobody can have *everything* they want *all* the time. And she knows how hard it can be to stay focused on her own life without getting distracted by what other people are buying and doing.

The principles in this book are timeless. The themes of budgeting, saving, staying out of debt, and giving are all things we've taught for decades. What's unique here is Rachel's approach. She's coming at these things from a totally fresh and different perspective, and I think it's a perspective the world needs today.

I believe Rachel Cruze is the perfect person to deliver this message to a culture that can't stop comparing their lives to what they see on Facebook, Instagram, and Pinterest, and I know this book can change your life. If you're tired of playing the comparison game and you're ready to focus on building the life *you* love, Rachel will show you how.

— Introduction —

I hate the sound of my alarm clock.

There I am, perfectly happy, content, and warm in my bed, just dreaming away when, out of nowhere, that annoying upbeat ring starts going off. My alarm jolts me out of dreamland and drops me into a new—and much too early—morning. It takes everything in me to not hit the snooze button or throw my phone across the room. I'm not even sure God's awake at 5:00 a.m., but I am. Now. Oh, how things have changed.

It wasn't always like this. Early in my career, I'd wake up around 7:00 a.m., roll out of bed, get ready in a rush, grab some coffee, and run out the door to get to work on time. Most mornings felt like a blur, and my body was basically on autopilot while my brain kept on snoozing. I didn't value or even enjoy that first hour of the day. My morning habit was simple: get up, get ready, and get out—as quickly as possible.

But my life's a lot different now. When I became a mom, I realized pretty quickly that if I wanted to have any time to myself at all during the day, I would have to get up early. The demands of being a wife, mother, speaker, writer, and frequent traveler can exhaust me if I don't secure a few precious moments of peace and quiet each morning. I need time to prepare for the day ahead of me by gathering my thoughts and enjoying a cup of coffee before my daughter wakes up and I have to get her and myself ready. If I skip that first part of my day, I don't feel as focused or productive. And if I tried to carve out some quiet time for myself later in the day, it would never happen. The only way for me to have this time was to create a new morning habit of getting up a couple of hours earlier than before.

That meant I would have to get up before the sun and get used to seeing 5:00 a.m. flashing on my phone's alarm. Getting up that early used to feel like a punishment. Now, it feels like a gift. I'll admit, the first few weeks of this new routine were a little rough. I was tired, I got mad at myself for staying up too late the night before, and I wasn't used to tiptoeing around the house in the dark. Over time, though, I grew to value those early morning hours. I liked how having that time made me feel. I felt more present with my husband, Winston, and our daughter. Now I don't even have to think about it. I just do it. It has become a habit for me.

LIVING WITH HABITS

People tend to have different reactions to the word *habit*. Some people think of habits in a negative light. Their minds immediately jump to "bad" habits like cracking knuckles, biting fingernails, or smacking gum. The thought of creating new habits may sound overwhelming, and the thought of breaking old, bad habits may sound intimidating. These people cringe when I bring up the idea of habits because they're naturally inclined to think I'm calling them out on something they need to change, and that sounds like a lot of work to them.

Other people see habits in a more positive light. They think of habits as healthy disciplines that enhance their lives. They view turning off their smartphone during dinner to focus on quality time with their family, saving up to pay cash for purchases, working out regularly, eating healthy food (most of the time, at least), setting the house alarm before walking out the door, and brushing their teeth at least twice a day all as good habits. These people light up when I talk about habits because they're always looking for some "life hack" to get where they want to go.

We All Have Habits

The word *habit* means acting or behaving in a usual or predictable way. It's what a person does on a regular basis. Habits are those things you do that you don't have to think hard about—an automated response to what's happening around you. My old morning routine (get up, get ready, get out) was definitely a habit. That's what I meant when I said I was on autopilot. The habit took over, so my body knew just what to do while my brain continued to snooze.

Charles Duhigg talks about this in his incredible book *The Power of Habit*. He writes, "When a habit emerges, the brain stops fully participating in decision making. It stops working so hard. . . . So unless you deliberately fight a habit . . . the pattern will unfold automatically."[1] When a choice is made consistently, it becomes a habit. And habits, according to Duhigg, are automatic. In other words, you don't even think about them.

For example, how hard do you have to think about each turn on your daily commute? How often do you get lost on your way to work or to your kids' school? I've driven the same route so much that my brain shuts down a little bit when it's time to drive to work. In fact, I had an experience like this not long ago. I needed to pick a few things up at our local warehouse store, which is located one street over from my office. Apparently, I completely zoned out while I was driving, because the next thing I knew, I was sitting in my office parking lot. In my normal parking spot. On a Saturday.

I laughed at myself when I came to my senses because I knew exactly what had happened. I was heading in the direction of my office, so my "drive to work" habit took over. Even though I was working on a book about money habits at the time, I was still surprised at how powerful that routine was. It made me realize how important it is not just to *be aware* of your habits but also to *take control* of them if you want to truly take control of your life.

Facing Our Money Habits

Habits affect every area of our lives, including our health, careers, relationships, and especially our money. We all have money habits. Some are good, and some are bad. Some take us closer to where we want to be, while others take us further and further away.

You may be in the habit of using cash for purchases, or you may instinctively grab a credit card from your wallet whenever you're in a checkout line. You may have a habit of talking to your spouse before making major purchases, or you may have an impulsive habit of hiding your purchases when you get home. Like it or not, our money habits impact our financial lives every single day. And, because of this, we've got to figure out how to harness the power of habit in order to live the lives we want.

That doesn't mean I always enjoy it when a healthy habit kicks in. I'm a natural spender. We'll talk more about that later, but, for now, I'll just admit that I love spending money. Some people are natural savers, and some people are natural spenders. Spending is my natural bent. However, I have some healthy money habits that keep my spending in check. So, when I walk through the doors of J.Crew and my natural impulse is to buy everything in sight, those instincts crash against my habits of not using debt, planning my spending, and talking to my husband about my purchases. Those are habits Winston and I have carefully added to our lives, and they're setting us up to live the life we want and do the things we value over the long term. So if occasionally feeling a little tension in J.Crew enables us to hit the goals we've set for ourselves, then sign me up!

The truth is, though, breaking bad money habits and replacing them with good ones is often easier said than done—especially if you don't realize how much your bad money habits are wrecking your life. I've talked to people who went years—even decades— going deeper and deeper into debt. When they wanted something, they just charged it with their credit card. It was an automatic response for them. They had no concept of the damage it was doing in their lives. Even if they suspected that there was a problem with their spending habits, they hadn't felt the pain to change. And without that little push, it can be incredibly difficult to come up with the emotional energy to change a long-standing habit.

But if you want to change your life, if you want to do the things you've always wanted to do, buy the things you've always wanted to buy, and go to the places you've always wanted to go to, then you're going to have to find that motivation to change your money habits. You need to aim the power of habit at the behaviors that will make your life better instead of tearing it apart one mistake at a time.

And don't worry about the mistakes you've made in the past. I'm not interested in beating you up for past mistakes. I want to encourage you to make wise choices and to build healthy habits moving forward. I can't promise it'll be easy, but I can promise it will lead to a happier, healthier, more peaceful life—a life without all the debt, stress, and worry that so many of our friends and family members are dealing with right now.

LET'S GET TO WORK

You have the opportunity to create the life you want. Though it may not feel like it right now, it's within reach—not thirty years from now, but right now. Change happens when you own up to the choices you make. If you don't like the outcomes you've created for yourself, such as debt, unhappiness, or dissatisfaction, then start making different choices that will create new habits in your life.

As we go through this book, I will shine a spotlight on the habits you need to take control of your money and to be able to afford the things you value. These money habits may not come easy to you and you may not get it right every time, but, as Larry Gelwix says, "Practice doesn't make perfect; practice makes permanent." And permanent, positive change is what we're after.

Some of the principles in this book may sound familiar. There's a reason for that. My dad, Dave Ramsey, has been teaching many of these things for decades. And before Dave Ramsey, there were financial giants like Larry Burkett, Howard Dayton, and Ron Blue teaching basic personal finance to everyday people. Ideas like staying out of debt, using cash for purchases, talking to your spouse about your money, and living on a budget aren't new, revolutionary ideas. The problem isn't that people haven't heard what to do; the real problem is that most people just don't do it. And in the age of one-click purchasing, social media pressure, online banking, and instant gratification, things are only getting worse.

I grew up with these principles. I've never used debt, and I learned at a young age to make a plan for my money. I know this stuff works, but the world has changed a little bit since Dad first started talking to people on the radio. This generation of young families is facing new pressures and temptations that our parents never had to deal with. Today's challenges and opportunities are uniquely ours, so let's figure out how to manage them together.

While I'd love to only be that friend who cheers you on, there are times when I'm going to have to be the friend who cares enough to tell you when you're going off track with your money. That means I'll be addressing some bad habits you may already have, because I know how easy it can be to allow bad habits to take you far off course.

As we get started, I have good news and bad news. The good news is that we're going to start with the one habit that has the power to change your financial life more than any other—and it's not what you think it is. The bad news is that it might slap you in the face with something you don't want to deal with quite yet. It might be a little tough, but it's a worthwhile journey. Breaking, building, and rebuilding habits can be hard work, but it's the only way to get to the life you've always dreamed of. You ready? Let's get to work!

— Habit 1 —

Quit the Comparisons

— 1 —

Comparisons Are Killing Us

Winston and I were in our second year of marriage. We were in our first career jobs making decent salaries, but nothing that out of the ordinary for a young couple a few years out of college. One night over dinner, we started talking about the future. We laughed and dreamed about the things we wanted to accomplish in our marriage, family, and careers.

During our conversation we talked about taking a trip to a place we'd never been before. We really hadn't gone anywhere together since our honeymoon, and the thought of a fancy getaway got us both excited. We were what some people call DINKs—dual-income, no kids—which meant we had some discretionary income to take a short trip together.

We had heard many great things about Charleston, South Carolina. Friends who had been there couldn't say enough good things about this storied coastal town. Once we priced out the flights and hotel, we realized we only had enough cash to cover an extended weekend, but that was fine. We were just excited to get away together for a few days.

We had a couple of months to save before the trip, so we squeezed every dollar we could out of our budget to put toward the getaway. We checked out all the restaurants online and made reservations, looked up fun things to do, and planned the weekend practically down to the minute. And, since Winston and I both stay incredibly busy at work, we agreed to make this a "no work, all play" trip. The day we finally left for South Carolina, I could feel months of stress roll off as the plane hit the air. It was time to relax!

Charleston, just in case you're wondering, was amazing. The food was outstanding. The people were friendly. It was everything people said it was and more—so much culture, elegance, and history. We didn't want to leave, but we had to come back to reality. So we decided then and there that this would be a place we would come back to again and again.

As soon as we got home, I plopped down on the couch and mindlessly scrolled through my Instagram feed. What better way to spend my afternoon than to catch up on my friends' foodie, baby, and cat pictures, right?

One of the first photos I saw was posted by a fashion blogger I follow—someone I don't know personally. She was on a trip to Europe that week. Not just Europe, but Greece. And not just Greece, but all the Greek isles. And, of course, she was sailing from one to another on this incredible yacht. Oh yes, I said *yacht*! The pictures showed it all: the unbelievable yacht, perfect setting, and most delicious-looking food I'd ever seen.

All I could think about was what it must feel like to walk in her shoes (which were probably all designer; hey there, Jimmy Choo) and live her life. Ever land on someone's feed and wish you were living their life in that moment? That was me. So, while scrolling through her pictures, with the warm glow of my fantastic trip to Charleston fading fast, I did what any normal, healthy person would do: I looked up airline tickets to Greece. No other vacation would do. It was Greece or bust!

I was already looking up the price of airline tickets before I snapped back to reality. We were newlyweds on a newlywed budget; we couldn't even afford to *get* to Greece, let alone pay for the resorts, excursions, and food. What's worse, Winston and I had just gotten back home from an amazing trip together. But instead of basking in the experience, all I could think about was how much better this person's trip was than mine.

Suddenly our fantastic trip to South Carolina seemed a little dull. And just like that, I had entered the comparison game. I was comparing a stranger's exciting vacation to the wonderful trip I had just taken with my husband and allowing her trip to steal my joy.

It took a little while to shake off the sudden need to go to Europe, but I thought about that whole experience for a long time after. Why had I let someone else's trip to Greece make me so anxious? What was it about *her* trip that made *my* trip feel inadequate? I had to come to terms with the fact that I was caught up in comparisons. I was chasing someone else's life instead of enjoying my own. I was letting someone I had never met influence not only how I was going to spend my money, but how I was going to live my life.

CHASING MAKE-BELIEVE

You would think I would have learned my lesson, but a few weeks later I was back at it again. This time I was captivated by pictures of a friend's remodeled kitchen. It was beautiful! Her kitchen looked like a home featured in a magazine or on one of those home improvement shows. The beautiful granite, the lights, and the cabinets—everything was perfectly coordinated. Without even realizing it, I started walking around my house planning what I needed to change immediately.

To make matters worse, I had actually just spent a little money updating the décor in our living room, and I was really happy with it. But then I saw what someone else had and felt the need to keep up. And it only took a split second for my thoughts to make that turn. Suddenly, I was comparing my home to hers, and I was no longer satisfied with what I had. After getting hit in the face with the comparison game twice in such a short time, I decided it was time to face the disgusting comparison monster head-on. I realized comparisons will not only steal our joy but our paychecks as well. If we don't get comparison living under control, we will constantly spend money just trying to keep up.

The Comparisons in Our Pockets

Comparison living is nothing new. I know that every generation in the history of the world has struggled with it to some degree or another. Hey, the instruction not to covet is even one of the Ten Commandments! But I really believe something has changed in the past ten years or so, and I believe it's tied to social media.

Thirty years ago, when my parents were my age, the term "keeping up with the Joneses" was pretty common. That was the mid-eighties, at what some would call the height of consumerism. If Dad came home and saw a brand-new car in the neighbor's driveway, he probably felt some urge to go get a nicer car himself. I get it. But here's what's different today: Back then, my parents had to actually be within eyeshot of the neighbors' new purchases. They had to see the Joneses' car *in person* before the comparison impulse kicked in. Today, however, we carry the Joneses around in our back pockets.

Our cell phones and social media apps are little windows into the lives of other people. If a friend on the other side of the world bought a new purse today, a picture of it could hit my phone before she ever even left the store. Despite all the value networks like Twitter, Instagram, and Facebook have brought into the world, there's one glaring negative that we have to face openly and honestly: these channels make it easier than ever for us to wish we were living someone else's life. And what I've come to realize is that when we start comparing ourselves to other people, we're playing a game we'll never win.

Better Than Reality

One of the most frustrating parts of social media is that it's not always real life. Most of what you see on Facebook and Instagram is enhanced. It's a public display of our *best* self. We usually put our best foot forward on social media and the pictures we post. Some people even go to the extreme, perfecting every detail. They take fifty different shots before posting the one, perfect, "candid" beach photo.

You scroll through your feed and see a picture of your coworker's brand-new car with the caption *#blessed*. This sudden urge to keep up overwhelms you. But comparing yourself to the proverbial Joneses is a dead end. You have to remember that the Joneses may actually be broke! What you are seeing isn't always the real story.

And I find it hilarious that no one ever posts a picture of their rusted, paid-for, '92 Camry on Facebook and tags it #blessed! Why? Because that trusty old car doesn't seem as exciting as a brand-new Tahoe.

Taking things one step further from reality, Instagram now offers the Joneses nearly two dozen different filters to make them look extra tan and any ocean they're laying beside look extra blue. It's probably safe to say we are all guilty of this! Hey, if it's a cold January afternoon and an Instagram filter can put a nice warm glow on my face, what's the harm? Thank you, Lo-Fi filter, for enhancing our reality.

Yes, there might be a picture in your social media feed that involves a family laughing while picnicking in the park. But what you don't see are the thirty-seven bad shots they deleted before they finally got that good one. I am guilty of this too. I don't want to put a goofy-looking picture of my daughter on Facebook. Of course not! I do all I can to get her to laugh. Then when I get the cute little grin I'm looking for, you better believe that's the picture I want to share with the world!

Here's the point: When you get caught up in social media comparisons, you're comparing yourself to make-believe. And when you compare yourself to make-believe, your real life will never feel good enough.

AM I GOOD ENOUGH?

Even though social media is probably the easiest place to compare, we can't forget about comparisons in real life and real time. Regardless of what stage of life you're in, it can seem impossible to avoid the comparison trap altogether. No matter what we do, where we go, or what we buy, someone is always there doing more, going further, and buying better. From jobs and houses to clothes and cars to schools and strollers (yes, people, even strollers)—the list goes on and on.

The Rat Race

What's weird is that this is true even if you're starting at the same place as someone else. When I think about the people I went to college with, I can see that we all kind of got off to the same start. Everyone's first job is at the bottom rung when it comes to salary and responsibilities. Because we're all in it together, it's like we emotionally lock arms with each other and do the work necessary to get ahead while making starter salaries. You're in your early twenties, and that's exactly where you're supposed to be in this stage of life.

But most people don't stay there for long. As you move out of the recent college graduate stage, situations and circumstances start to change. Some people rapidly progress through their careers. Others seem to stay stagnant longer than others. Some get married. Some have kids early and leave the workforce. Some never seem to advance personally or professionally, and they act like they're still in college. And as a result of that, incomes and lifestyles begin to change.

Bigger houses, exotic vacations, expensive jewelry, and fancy cars start filling up our social media feeds. We think, *How can they afford that car? They make the same salary as I do!* or *They're going to Disney again? We haven't even been once!* Somehow, our friends' lives start to look better than ours, and that nagging sense of comparison creeps into our thinking. It changes our attitudes and, just as sadly, our relationships with the people we're comparing ourselves to.

Competitive Parenting

Once you bring kids into the picture, it's a whole new ball game. When I told a good friend we were pregnant, one of her first comments was, "Welcome to the world of comparisons." I had no idea how true this would be. The comparisons among pregnant friends began immediately. "Are you sick? Do you actually throw up, or do you just feel nauseated?" Oh yes, some women compare how bad their morning sickness is. But it didn't stop there. Other gems included:

"Are you still working out?" (Translation: "How much weight have you gained?")

"Have you registered for baby gifts yet? Where? No, not there! You need to register *here* instead."

"What kind of stroller did you get?"

"Did you get your baby furniture at Pottery Barn Kids, or did you just go with the cheap stuff?"

After nine months of this, I thought I'd experienced the worst of it. I found out just how wrong I was the instant our daughter, Amelia, was born. Practically the day we brought her home, we were hit with what can best be called "competitive parenting." *Has your baby rolled over? Can she hold her head up yet? Has she walked? Is she sleeping through the night? Oh, that's the stroller you decided to go with? Did your baby smile at four weeks? Because mine did. Are you nursing? What preschool is your child going to? She hasn't started crawling yet?* Insanity.

Every question makes you feel inadequate, like you're doing something wrong. And the cycle of comparison continues.

Looking at Each Other

Even our daily routines are filled with comparisons. It starts on Sunday. There is that family in your small group who pulls into the parking space beside you at church. When they get out, there isn't a wrinkle in sight. Designer and boutique clothes are all coordinating. Makeup and hair are perfect. Their kids are so well-behaved. Suddenly you feel like you aren't doing enough.

Then Monday morning comes around and you're sitting in the carpool line waiting to drop your child off at school. You can see your reflection in the shine of the luxury car in front of you, and you notice how put together the kids are as they pop out of the car. When you get to work, your coworker tells you all about his exciting weekend of late nights with friends and fancy food. Before you've even had your first cup of coffee, you're wondering why you can't get your life together and have what other people have. And that's when you ask yourself, *Does this ever end?*

The answer, my friend, is no. No, it doesn't. But you can put an end to it for yourself. Yes, you can move past the comparisons that may be killing you right now. It's possible!

THE CURE BEGINS WITHIN

I'm afraid it's time for a little tough love. You ready? Here it is. Comparing ourselves to others is essentially a coping mechanism for our own insecurities. We believe we don't measure up so we project our insecurity onto others. We are insecure about how we look, how our kids are dressed, how our houses are decorated, and so on. And it's those insecurities—our own internal struggles—that are keeping us from living the kind of life we love. We can't blame social media, and we can't blame the Joneses. They're doing the same thing we are, just trying to figure out how to love their lives. Once you take your focus off of them and put it back onto your own life, you can start to turn things around with your life and money.

Clearing Our Vision

As we compare our lives to other people, we fall into a dangerous trap. We make assumptions about other people's lives and situations, and those assumptions are often wrong (or at least incomplete).

You know that "laughing in the park" family we talked about earlier? They may seem to have the most incredible life. They may be the family that seems to have it all together based on the school their kids attend, their house, and the amazing beach vacations they take with their kids three times a year. And you know this because they post all the pictures on Facebook. Sure, you know the family I'm talking about. We *all* know that family. Everything seems just perfect for them.

What we may not stop to consider, though, is that there's a chance their marriage is stressed. They may have no margin with

11

their money because their paycheck comes in and goes right back out in payments. They may have no margin with their time because he works 24/7 just to keep up the appearance of the "perfect" life.

But the other side of the coin is true as well. This is where I'm sometimes guilty. I can see a picture of that family on a gorgeous vacation—usually around the same time I am craving a vacation myself—and I immediately think, *Sure, they look happy, but I bet they aren't. I bet they couldn't even pay for that vacation with cash. They probably charged everything on their credit card. They're probably over there yelling at each other right now.*

Guilty as charged. But the truth is, we have no idea what's going on behind the scenes in anyone else's family—unless they tell us, of course. They really could be the happiest, healthiest, wealthiest family in the world. Or they could be broke, miserable, and one fight away from divorce. Or, more likely, they're somewhere in the middle. We just don't know. We can't know. So our assumptions— good or bad—are meaningless. They don't change the other family's situation, and they don't change our situation. It's a waste of energy, and, frankly, it's none of our business.

A PROBLEM WE MAKE FOR OURSELVES

I believe the game of comparisons is a problem of our own making. These are pressures we put on ourselves. We spend so much money, time, energy, and attention trying to bridge a gap that doesn't even exist.

You may have been a little uncomfortable reading this chapter. Trust me, it was uncomfortable for me to write a lot of it! But I'm done with denial. The truth is, most of us deal with comparisons each and every day. It doesn't make us bad people. It doesn't mean we're selfish or jealous or envious of our friends. It just means we're human. We can't blame ourselves for the thoughts that pop into our heads, but we *can* take responsibility for what we do with those thoughts. Are we going to nurture the comparisons and wallow in our own discontentment, or are we going to stop those thoughts in their tracks and enjoy the life in front of us?

It's a struggle sorting through all of the thoughts and feelings we have about others and the lives they are living, but if we really want to love our own lives, we've got to come face to face with the bad habits that are holding us back. We are spending money we may or may not have just to keep up with a life we think we are missing out on. And that is ruining not only our emotional lives but our financial lives as well.

As a culture, I truly believe we've made a habit of comparing our lives to others, and it is time to break that habit. We'll talk about how to do that in the next chapter.

2

Blessed vs. #blessed

There is a fascinating phenomenon repeating itself on social media these days, and we've all seen it. It's there, lurking at the end of half the posts you see online. It's the smiley, happy exclamation point at the end of a friend's latest post about her fantastic vacation. Most of the time, you can see it coming before you get to the end of the photo caption. It's the latest weapon in the comparison-driven war of one-upmanship currently being waged on your favorite social networks. Yes, you know what's coming. I'm talking about #blessed.

"Look at what my amazing husband gave me for our anniversary! #blessed"

"Honored to accept my new position as Executive Vice President of Sales for a Fortune 500 company. #blessed"

"I can't believe this view out my new bedroom window! #blessed"

"Jetting off to Hawaii for a long weekend! #blessed"

"I've always wanted a Lexus! #blessed"

"Oh, he shouldn't have! #blessed"

And the pictures—oh, the pictures. Amazing sunsets. Feet in the sand. Six-pack abs. Rooftop pools. First-class airline seats. #blessed #ilovehimsomuch #treatingmyself #YOLO

I'll be the first to admit that I've been guilty of using #blessed in the past, but once I became more aware of this habit of comparison living, I started paying more attention to when, where, and why people throw in that little hashtag. And, almost every time I see it now, I translate it as a humble brag.

Am I saying that everyone who uses #blessed means to imply that? No way. I know some of the sweetest, most caring, and generous people in the world. There's no way that's what they mean to say. There are others, though, who know *exactly* what they're implying with it. We can't control that. All we can control is what our response is when we see it. If we seriously want to develop a habit of quitting the comparisons, we've got to take control of our thoughts and reactions to other people's stuff and success. We need to choose *real* blessings and let go of someone else's #blessed. So how do we do that?

HOW TO QUIT THE COMPARISONS

Quitting comparisons is an easy thing to say, but it's no easy thing to do. It can be tough to identify clear steps to win. I haven't figured it all out yet; after all, this is something I'm still working on myself. However, I *can* share with you some specific steps I've taken and principles I've applied to my own life to help me take my eyes off of other people and put them back on creating the life I want to live for myself.

Step 1: Change Your Perspective

In the last chapter we said that what we see on social media doesn't always reflect reality. It's usually not the complete picture of someone's life; it's the highlight reel. That's true for other people, and, if we're being honest, it's true for us as well. It's not only a social media issue, however. Our perception of reality can be just as skewed in real life.

Stuff Doesn't Equal Wealth

One of the most surprising lessons I learned as a teenager is that nice stuff doesn't always equal wealth. Once, when a group of girls from school decided to go to a concert together, one girl in our circle of friends said she couldn't go. She couldn't afford the $100 ticket. Now, don't get me wrong—paying $100 for a concert ticket in high school was a big deal. I had to do hours of babysitting to earn that money! What surprised me, though, is that this friend drove a brand-new luxury car. She wore designer clothes, and her family lived in a super-nice house in an expensive neighborhood. I just couldn't wrap my head around the fact that this girl, who looked like she could do anything she wanted, couldn't afford a concert ticket.

I talked to my mom about it that night. "Mom, how could she not afford a ticket?" I asked. "She's rich!"

My mom stopped what she was doing, looked me in the eye, and said something I'll never forget: "Rachel, that's what debt does. It makes people look better off than they actually are." Just because someone *looks* wealthy doesn't mean they actually are. This may or may not have been my friend's situation in high school, but

17

someone's nice car, fancy jewelry, and giant house could all be based on debt. The show on the outside may not match the truth on the inside. The lesson there for me was that things aren't always what they appear to be.

Don't get me wrong. I'm definitely not saying that everyone who has nice things uses debt to get them. A few years ago, a friend confided in me that she and her husband were in major financial trouble. They weren't careless with their money, but life had dealt them a tough blow. She was a teacher, and he had recently lost his job. They were barely getting by on her teacher's salary. Every time I saw her, however, she was wearing a new pair of expensive yoga pants. It may sound silly, but this really started bothering me. I told Winston, "I can't believe she has so many pairs of those pants! They can't afford to spend that much on something so trivial. What are they thinking?"

Soon after, she and I were hanging out with some other friends. I overheard her telling someone else that some of her students' moms had pooled their money and given her three pairs of those pants for Christmas. She went on and on about how grateful she was for the gift because it gave her the chance to have something nice for herself while she and her husband were facing such difficult money troubles. I felt terrible. I had judged her for something that wasn't even true. It was another hard lesson that you can't always trust your assumptions.

Wealth Doesn't Equal Stuff

Another interesting truth in this is that having wealth doesn't necessarily mean you have nice stuff. We all have ideas of what millionaires look like and how they live, but that's usually based on unrealistic assumptions or television's portrayal of "rich people." The truth is, people who are actually wealthy live a lot differently than you might expect.

The late Thomas J. Stanley wrote a fabulous book called *The Millionaire Next Door*. He spent years studying the behaviors of the average millionaire (someone with a net worth of a million dollars or more). He meticulously reviewed their lifestyles and concluded that these successful men and women look more like "regular people" and not at all like the fancy, well-dressed, well-to-do rich people you see on TV.

One of the things he discovered was that the average millionaire drives a two-year-old or older car. Why? Because when you have as much money as they do, you don't care what other people think! As Stanley interviewed these millionaires, a high percentage talked about how they drove used cars and lived in modest homes. They weren't flashy and were pretty conservative in their spending. It was refreshing to read and a good reminder that, again, things aren't always as they seem.

Step 2: Cheer Each Other On

I love working at my dad's company, Ramsey Solutions. We do important work, and we get to help people all over the country take control of their money and get out of debt. Some of the success stories we hear blow me away! The really cool part, though, is the way the team members celebrate each other's progress.

You may think that everyone in our office is debt-free, but that's not true. Our team members represent every stage of the financial spectrum. We may all be at different places on the journey, but we're all heading in the same direction. So, we have some millionaires on the team, and we have some people who are fighting through tens of thousands of dollars in debt. And, of course, we have a lot of people somewhere in between. We all dress pretty casually, so it's hard to tell who's doing well and who's struggling under a pile of student loans. But the one place you can really get a sense of our variety is in the parking lot.

When you pull in, you will likely see a few Lexus and Mercedes models, along with several other really nice cars. You will *also* see a

1980 Chevy Nova with duct tape, rust, and a mix-and-match paint job. But the person getting out of the Mercedes doesn't look down on the person driving the Nova. In fact, it's exactly the opposite. They cheer that person on because they know how hard they're fighting and of the sacrifices they're making to get out of debt.

The guy in the Nova doesn't roll his eyes at the people who drive nicer, newer cars either. Again, it's the opposite. He doesn't plan to drive it forever; he looks at the people in the newer cars as huge encouragements, as a sign of where he wants to be himself. There's no comparison game going on here. Instead, we're all cheering each other on. It's an incredible attitude that you can adopt yourself, even if everyone around you doesn't. But you can't do it if you're always comparing your life to other people's. Constantly comparing ourselves to others prevents us from cheering on those who are working hard to get somewhere and celebrating with those who have made it there.

So here's the challenge: When a friend tells you about her new job, be happy for her. If someone buys a new house, show some excitement. If someone shares some great news with you, keep the focus on them instead of turning it back to yourself. Find big and small ways to celebrate other people's accomplishments. That's one way we get to show love and support to others. It's like the Bible says, "Rejoice with those who rejoice" (Romans 12:15). Don't feel like you're losing just because someone else is winning. Their success has nothing to do with you, so celebrate *their* success sincerely while you keep working toward *your own*.

Step 3: Stop Looking at Your Parents

My parents live in a beautiful home. Seriously, it's amazing. They have worked hard and have been responsible with money for decades, and I'm so proud that they're now able to enjoy what they've worked so hard for. You know what I *don't* do when I look at their house?

I don't try to figure out how I can buy the one next door. At this point in my life, that's just not going to happen.

Mom and Dad have a thirty-year head start on Winston and me. We may get where they are one day, but we aren't there today. The same may be true for you too. And yet so many people graduate college, get married, start their careers, and immediately expect to be able to live the same kind of lifestyle as their parents. It's crazy! Why in the world should someone with a starter salary assume they can live just as well as their hard-working, almost-retired parents? Answer: they shouldn't.

Winston and I try to keep this in perspective, but it isn't always easy. Sure, the big things like houses or cars are easier to keep a handle on, but I still get tripped up on the little things sometimes. A few years into my career, I went out to eat with my parents and noticed a beautiful new purse my mom had just bought. I told her how gorgeous it was and that I wished I could get one just like it. Without really thinking much about it, she said sweetly, "Oh sure, honey! You should buy one for yourself!"

When I got home from dinner, I went online to order it and saw the price. Yikes! To say it was out of my "newlywed, only-worked-three-years-in-the-real-world" budget would be an understatement. At that point, it really hit me that I was still in my early twenties. While I had been working hard for those three years, it didn't grant me the right to go buy whatever I wanted. I needed to live like I was in my early twenties—not like I was in my early fifties. Comparing ourselves to our peers is bad enough, but comparing ourselves to people decades further along in their careers and wealth building is just ridiculous.

Step 4: Redefine "I Deserve It"

One of the biggest dangers in comparing ourselves to others is the spirit of entitlement it can create. We see someone else's success and think, *I work harder than he does. I should have what he has. I deserve it.*

Deserve is a dangerous word, and it gets people into more trouble than they'd ever expect—or care to admit. The belief that the world owes us something is why so many of us live in a constant state of dissatisfaction and jealousy.

I fall into this trap at times. I start to tell myself why I deserve something—or better—why I should have the same or better than someone else. I tell myself, *Rachel, you work so hard. You deserve a nice vacation. You need newer clothes than what you have in your closet.*

Whenever I do this, I'm having a classic Veruca-Salt-from-Willy-Wonka-style tantrum. I might as well stomp my feet and scream, "I want it! I want it right now!" It's hard to admit that I do that occasionally, but I do. And these pity parties are almost always when I'm alone in my car or by myself at home. They usually happen in my head and last for about half an hour before I snap out of it and back to reality. Maybe—just maybe—I'm not the only one?

I have to stop in those times and remind myself that I don't *deserve* anything. The only things I *deserve* to buy are what Winston and I plan for and pay cash for. That's it. Period. If it's not part of our plan and we don't have the cash on hand, we make it a goal to work toward in the future. I have to remind myself that having it right this second isn't an option, so I just need to move on. How's that for a pep talk?

Step 5: Own Your Stuff

Growing up, I always heard my parents say, "It's okay to have nice stuff; just don't let your nice stuff have you." What they meant is that we sometimes give in to the pursuit of stuff for the wrong reasons. People make bad decisions and go into debt for things they don't need and can't afford. Then, once they have the thing they think will make them happy, they get distracted by something else and start chasing after it instead. The end result of this is a big pile of nice stuff with a lot of debt and misery attached.

The road of comparisons always dead-ends at debt. Remember, it's okay to have nice things. There's nothing wrong with enjoying a little luxury as long as it makes sense in your world. However, when you pile up a bunch of stuff and go neck-deep into debt to buy it all, you don't really own your stuff; it owns you. The debt takes over, steals all your income, and you suddenly become a servant to the things you thought would make you happy.

We'll talk a lot more about debt and wise spending later. For now, I just encourage you to examine your buying motives before you make a purchase. If your identity and your life's worth are wrapped up in what you're buying, you are setting yourself up for disaster.

THE CURE FOR COMPARISONS

Too many people allow cultural expectations—that is, *other people*— to dictate their own values and family priorities. I've been there too. I know it's an empty and endless battle to try to keep up. You feel like a hamster on a wheel, running as hard and fast as you can and ultimately going nowhere. Doing that for a lifetime will leave you completely exhausted. But your life doesn't have to look like that. There is hope; there is an antidote. There is one and only one cure to comparison living, and that is contentment.

What Contentment Looks Like

In our book *Smart Money Smart Kids*, my dad and I make the point that content people don't always *have* the best of everything, but they *make* the best of everything. Contentment isn't a place you get to financially; it's a place you get to emotionally and spiritually.

It's a peace in your spirit that knows what you have, no matter how much or how little, is *enough*. Contentment is the inner determination to be happy and fulfilled wherever you are with whatever you have. The apostle Paul put it like this: "I have learned to be content whatever the circumstances" (Philippians 4:11). And, yes, I know this is a lot easier said than done.

I wish I could give you specific steps to take to guarantee your contentment, but I can't. I will tell you the two big secrets to living a contented life, but before we get there, let's take a look at what a content person looks like. You may realize that you have some of these people around you already. You may even realize that you are one yourself!

Content People Are Satisfied

Contentment allows you to be in a state of joy and satisfaction. You are happy with where you are in life. That doesn't mean you don't have goals for the future or that you aren't working toward being a better person tomorrow than you are today. It definitely doesn't mean that you're stagnant or apathetic, or that you're choosing to sit around and do nothing new, exciting, and challenging with your life. It just means that you have a peace about your life and a sincere enjoyment about what you have *today* without basing all your happiness on what you hope to achieve *tomorrow*.

Since we're talking about comparisons, I will give you one big tip here: It's almost impossible to be satisfied with your own life if you're constantly looking at what someone else has. If you're struggling to appreciate the blessings in your life and if you're constantly distracted by the #blessings of other people, it may be time to put some blinders on for a little while.

Shut off the social networks. Stop strolling through the mall. Unsubscribe from all those email newsletters and advertisements that try to convince you how much you're missing. Spend that time and energy focusing on how much you truly have. Look at your family, your friends, your home, your job, and all the things in your life that really matter. Then rejoice in all you have.

Content People Are at Peace

Comparisons bring discontentment, and discontentment brings anxiety. Have you ever noticed how stressed you start to feel when you're focused on other people's stuff? That happens to me every now and then, like when I was scrolling through that fashion blogger's Greek isles pictures after my Charleston trip. If you ever find your mood changing while you're on social media, that may be a sign that you need to back off for a while.

Focusing on the blessings in your own life helps you get past all that. When you are content, you have a peace about your life. You may not be where you want to be yet, but you're comfortable about where you're heading. And, just as important, you're able to be comfortable with where *someone else* is heading too. That's when you become the kind of friend who can genuinely celebrate someone else's victories and accomplishments. Don't we love the friends who will be happy for us? Don't we avoid the friends we know will try to put a dark cloud over our heads? When we're at peace with our lives, our relationships get better because we become the kind of friend other people want to have.

Content People Save More and Avoid Debt

This one may be a no-brainer, but content people aren't interested in burying themselves under a pile of debt in order to buy stuff they think will make them happy. And, since they aren't trying to one-up other people, they usually save more and build wealth over the long haul. It's kind of ironic, isn't it? Those who seem least interested in the *appearance* of wealth are often the ones who build the most wealth over time. Funny how that works, isn't it?

Content People Are Generous

Generosity is the most attractive character trait you can imagine. People who freely give their time, energy, attention, sympathy, encouragement, and, yes, their money, are the kind of people you want to spend time with. Generosity makes us so much more of who we want to be! It's hard to realize, then, that a lot of the comparison-based decisions we make every day take us further and further away from this ideal.

When we're busy investing all our attention and money into keeping up with the Joneses, we usually don't have enough left to invest in other people and worthy causes. When you get to the place where you are satisfied with what you have, you realize you have plenty left to give to others. We'll talk more about giving later.

The Two Keys to Contentment: Gratitude and Humility

So how do you work toward a life of contentment? I believe it starts with a grateful heart. There is no room for discontentment in a heart filled with gratitude. As my friend Chris Hogan often says, "It's hard to be hateful when you're grateful!" That's why it's such a good idea to stop often and take inventory of all the incredible blessings in our lives.

A local pastor recently hit this message pretty hard in a sermon series. He challenged his church to focus on the issue of gratitude by posting to social media five things they were grateful for every day for a week. It's a big church, and the response was huge! I have a lot of friends and coworkers who go to this church, so my social feeds were blowing up with these gratitude posts. Posts covered everything from kids to health to jobs. One friend even posted, "I am thankful for being tired and sore, because that means I have two legs that allow me to run." I loved seeing these posts, probably because the spirit about them was so genuine. These were real, heartfelt notes of thanksgiving. I didn't see any trace of the #blessed vibe at all!

And to start making gratitude part of my daily routine, one of the first things I do each day is open up the notes app on my phone and list two things I'm grateful for. It's become one long scrolling list by now, and I love going back through it and reminding myself of all the incredible things God's given me or done for me. At the end of a long day, especially if it's been stressful or I'm worried about something, I'll pull up that list and scroll through it. Taking the time to think through the blessings in my life changes my whole outlook. It's a fantastic way to start and end the day.

So the first key to contentment is gratitude, and the second key grows out of that grateful heart. I'm talking about humility. But what is humility? I believe C. S. Lewis said it best: "Humility is not thinking less of yourself, but thinking of yourself less." I love that quote. Too often, humility gets a bad rap. Many people equate humility with weakness or self-diminishment. That's not what it is at all.

You can be humble and still recognize your strengths, talents, and accomplishments. You don't have to beat yourself up to be humble. In fact, that's a pretty unhealthy approach, and it's one of the biggest dangers of comparison living. The more we compare ourselves to others, the less we think of ourselves. That's a dangerous trap we've got to avoid.

True humility is just thinking of ourselves less often. It means not trying to make ourselves the star of the show, not flaunting our successes to the world, and not feeding our egos by making a big deal of ourselves. When we get this right, we're on our way to genuine contentment. Then we can celebrate and encourage each other, we can cheer each other on, and we can actually be proud of someone else's success because we aren't threatened by it. That's such a great place to be, and that's the kind of people the world needs more of.

Know What You Value

One of the biggest stumbling blocks to achieving true contentment—and one of the biggest problems with comparisons—is that we allow other people to define our values. The point of this book is to learn the money habits that will enable you to live the life *you* want. In order to do that, you've got to know what you value. That's right—what *you* value, not what your friends value and not what the culture says you *should* value. Your values are up to you, but too many people never take the time to figure out what's really important to them. They just go with the flow and chase the life everyone else is chasing without ever stopping to ask what *they* want for themselves.

Every individual and every family is going to have a different set of values. That's what makes us all unique! If everyone were the same, with the same interests, same jobs, same clothes, and so on, this world would be a seriously boring place to live. But it's not boring, is it? That's because we live in a world of variety. There are an endless number of things to do, places to go, and experiences to have. I, for one, believe it's time to not only define our personal values, but to rejoice in them as well!

Since this is a book about *money* habits, let's get more specific. All of your money decisions will flow out of what's important to you. Your career choices, purchases, investments, college selections for the kids—everything. For example, let's say you value having a job you love, but the career you've chosen pays a relatively small salary. Is it worth less money to love what you're doing? No one else can decide that for you; it's up to you and you alone.

Two of my best friends are in this place right now. He is a teacher and loves what he does. She values staying at home with their kids. They know that, because of these decisions, they will have a limited lifestyle and will have to live financially lean. It's not always easy for them, living a life where going out to eat, getting her nails done, and going on vacation with friends are rare. However, that's the choice they've made for themselves based on what is important for them, and they are completely happy with the choice they've made. That's awesome!

Another couple we know is making a different choice. He makes an impressive income in sales, but he isn't that passionate about what he does. She works outside the home, too, but she isn't crazy about her job. Neither of them hate what they're doing; they just don't love it. However, they value other things above job satisfaction. They are working on getting out of debt because they've decided they want to be a debt-free family. Once they're debt-free, they want to take exciting family trips and move to a better school system for their kids. They dream about an early retirement with plenty of cash on hand to do whatever they want. Since they value those things, they've made the decision to stay in their good-paying jobs. The income they earn enables them to focus on the things they really value, and they're happy with that decision. That's awesome too!

Another one of my girlfriends made yet a different choice. She was a missionary in Africa for a couple of years and absolutely loved it. Her lifestyle wasn't anywhere close to what it would be if she had been living and working here in the States, but she didn't care. She was doing what she loved and she was totally fulfilled in that calling. Just like the others I've mentioned, she's living out her values and is perfectly content.

I love these stories, and I love how these three families have taken a financial stand based on their personal values. They know that gratitude drives humility and humility drives contentment. And, because of this, they are some of the happiest, most fulfilled people I know.

TAKE BACK CONTROL OF YOUR LIFE

Every dollar you spend is a reflection of your values. If that's true (and it is), why on earth would we hand those decisions over to any-one else? And yet that's exactly what we're doing when we indulge the comparisons. We're handing someone else the steering wheel, and we're taking a back seat in our own lives. It's time to take that control back!

If you really want to win with money, it's time to get serious about the inner voices and dissatisfaction you may face when you see someone else's life. You have to take a hard look at yourself and figure out why you're so interested in what someone else is getting or doing. Their life won't change yours. No one else can hand you your values. You have to figure that out for yourself. And, once you do, you'll be prepared to arrange your life in the pursuit of those values.

I know I started this book with what might be the hardest of all the money habits, but I truly believe this is the critical first step. If you want to get out of debt, live on a budget, communicate well about money, build wealth, spend wisely, and give generously, you've got to first focus on the things *you* value. And that means you've got to quit the comparisons.

Steer Clear of Debt

3

Debt Is a Dead End

I don't know if I want them to come over. Should we just meet them at a restaurant?"

This was the question I asked Winston after we made plans for a couple we knew to come over for dinner. I was hesitant and worried—not because of the couple who was coming for dinner, but because we barely had any furniture in our house. Not very secure of me, huh?

When Winston and I moved to Nashville, we were your typical newlyweds starting out with just a little money to furnish our new home.

If you have ever spent time furniture shopping, you might be able to understand my shock when I learned just how expensive furniture can be. I had been living as a college student with dorm room furniture for four years, so I didn't realize how much quality furniture costs. I wish I could say I played it cool when we went into the furniture store to look, but I didn't. I remember staring blankly at the sales lady as she told me the price of the couch I was looking at on the showroom floor. I may or may not have laughed out loud and said, "No, I wasn't asking the price for five couches, just one!"

It was difficult because I was done with the hand-me-down furniture from my college days. I really wanted to step up to nice furniture and not fill up our house with cheap stuff we would have to replace a year later. Because of that choice, we could only afford to buy a few basic pieces. So, if you had walked through our house at that time, you would have seen that it was nearly empty. There was enough for the two of us to be comfortable, but that was about it. So the thought of having someone over for dinner freaked me out.

I remember being so insecure about it. Most of the friends we had made in Nashville were older than us and more established. They all had cute homes that were full of nice furniture, beautiful décor, and every kitchen appliance you could think of. From the moment our dinner guests walked into our home, I started explaining why we didn't have a lot of stuff. They kept smiling, laughing, and reassuring me it was fine. Honestly, they didn't care—they just wanted to hang out with us.

Most of the expectations you think people have of you simply don't exist; these are expectations you put on yourself. Even so, when the couple left that night, I was still a little embarrassed. That was one of the first times I understood why people go into debt. I remember thinking how easy it would be to just go to the furniture store, open up a credit account, and get all the furniture and décor we wanted. It definitely would have scratched the furniture itch I was having at the moment.

WHAT IS DEBT?

I grew up in a family where debt was a four-letter word. My parents hated debt, and for good reason. Back before my dad was the debt-hating, credit-card-cutting Dave Ramsey America knows today, he was a young guy in real estate who had several properties and a lot of debt associated with them. By the time he was twenty-six, he had a $1 million net worth. But Dad's entire business was built around about $3 million of debt. One day, the bank called all his loans, and he couldn't pay them back. He says today that he was trying to "out-earn his stupidity," but that couldn't last forever. Eventually, all that debt crashed down on top of my parents.

From Renting to Owning What I Believe

I was born the year they declared bankruptcy. That means I've spent my life watching my parents figure out how money works by using common sense and the money principles found in the Bible.

Coming out of bankruptcy, Mom and Dad vowed to never go back into debt. It left a scar on their lives and marriage. My parents were determined to raise my sister, brother, and me with the knowledge of *how* to live debt-free, along with the *commitment* to actually do it. So I can say that staying debt-free is a choice that Winston and I make on a daily basis. It has always been an absolute in my mind, and I will never cross that line.

This was my mind-set because of how my parents raised me, sure, but I eventually took it on for myself. You could say I went from *renting* my parents' strong principles about money to *owning* those beliefs for myself. My decision to live debt-free is no longer because "Mom and Dad told me to" but because it is a choice I have made for my life. Sure, I *could* go out today and lease a car, get three credit cards, and finance a houseful of furniture. But I won't. I have lived by this simple money habit: if I don't have the money, I don't buy it.

Occasionally, people try to challenge my credibility because of that stand. I guess I understand that, but I certainly don't agree with it. I don't need to be an alcoholic to know drinking too much can harm you. I don't need to do drugs to know that behavior can wreck your life. In the same way, I don't need to be in debt to understand the stress and pain it causes people. I have learned you don't have to make devastating mistakes with your money to learn how to handle it well.

Not only do I choose to live a debt-free life, but I really despise debt as well. As in, I *hate* it. That's partly because of the pain it caused my parents, but it's also because I see the pain it causes so many other people. I never see peace in the eyes of someone who has a wallet full of credit cards, a pile of student loans, and two SUV-sized car loans. Instead, I see fear. Because of that, I detest debt with a passion.

So I was surprised at myself when I was standing in our barely furnished home and thought for a second how easy it would be to go out and get the furniture we wanted with low monthly payments for the next few years. In that moment I suddenly understood why debt is so appealing. I had to learn to be secure, happy, and content with what Winston and I had and with what we could afford to buy with cash. If I didn't, I would have missed out on so much joy because I was worried about something as shallow as furniture. We didn't go into debt to get the rest of our furniture, but it did take almost two years to finally have our house looking just like we wanted it to. I remember experiencing such satisfaction after we finally added our final piece: a dining room table and chairs (which I got on sale, thank you very much).

I tell you this story because I want you to know it's possible for you too. It's possible to live the life you want and love that life without using debt. It's possible to finally start living life on your terms and with your own money.

Defining Debt

One of my favorite aspects of my job is meeting people from all walks of life and from all over the country. I especially love talking to people after a speaking event. I love hearing their stories— hearing about the victories and struggles they have with money. Unfortunately their stories usually involve debt. One college-aged guy approached me and said, "I don't have debt." "Way to go!" I told him. "Good for you! Tell me. How are you getting through college without debt?"

I thought he'd say something about the scholarships and grants that he had landed, or that he and his parents started saving for college when he was young, or that he was working two jobs while going to school. Instead, he said, "Well, I do have student loans, but I don't have debt."

I politely responded, "Sorry, but that means you *do* have debt. Student loans are debt." He and I talked for a bit longer, and the fact that his student loans would follow him after college slowly started to sink in. That conversation reminded me that I can't always assume when I talk to people that we're speaking the same language. You can't be debt-free . . . except for the student loans. You can't be debt-free . . . except for the car lease. There's no good debt and bad debt. You're either debt-free or you're not.

Just so we're clear, let me give you a simple definition of debt. *Debt is owing anything to anyone for any reason.* It's that simple. Credit cards? Debt. A car loan? Debt. A student loan? Debt. That's all debt. I don't want you to miss this, because if we can't agree on what debt is and what it is not, then the rest of this book will get confusing.

In order to live the life you want to live and love it, debt can't be part of your plan. You might be shaking your head at me right now. You might believe that debt is a tool to get where you want to go. With it, you can go on vacation, buy the clothes you like, and drive the car you want. And you can do all of this without having the money to pay for it in the moment and without having to wait a long time to save.

And in that sense, it's true. Debt allows you to have whatever you want immediately. But you have to realize the long-term implications of choosing to finance your present with your future. Debt steals the very thing that helps you win with money—your income. When you have debt, you don't get to decide what you do with your money. Your lenders decide that for you. You can't choose to take your money and save it, invest it, spend it, or even give it away. You lose the ability to make choices about your money when you have debt.

There isn't just a financial toll to having debt; there is an emotional toll as well. When you owe someone money—whether it is the bank, a credit card company, or a family member—it changes the way you live. It changes the reason you go to work. It creates such a burden for you that sometimes it seems hard to breathe. And while you may be tired and weary of the debt lifestyle, you're not sure how to do it any other way.

If you're experiencing those feelings now, keep reading. We'll get there.

DEBT'S DECEPTION

Debt always keeps us in the past and prevents us from focusing on our future. After all, it's hard to see beyond the next thirty days when you're worried about how you're going to cover all the household bills. You see, adopting a lifestyle of debt means you'll be managing your debt, not your money. This trap is so easy to fall into that many people don't realize they have a problem until they're in over their heads.

Debt's Broken Promises

If there is one thing I've observed about debt, it's this: debt is full of broken promises. Debt confuses the make-believe world of what we want or think we deserve with the truth about what we can actually afford. And when we blur the lines between reality and fantasy, we're in dangerous territory.

Proverbs 22:7 says, "The borrower is slave to the lender." You'll never see that referenced in any credit card advertisement, payday loan commercial, or student loan document. And, honestly, I haven't heard it in many sermons either! But that doesn't make it any less true. Our culture tells us debt is the key that unlocks the door to endless happiness, joy, and satisfaction. Yet nothing could be further from the truth. Debt will always deliver just the opposite. Debt will always leave you stressed, frustrated, and simply wanting more.

Most people don't intentionally set out to go thousands or tens of thousands of dollars into debt. They just passively take on more and more debt, never thinking about what they're giving up in the process. Soon they realize they've handed over the reins of their lives to bills that come every thirty days. They don't even realize how much control debt has over them until they are so far in that they can't dig out.

Two Mind-sets That Will Keep You in Debt

How does debt creep into our lives so easily? I believe this has to do with two mind-sets that our culture has come to accept as normal.

First—and I hear this all the time—is the mind-set that some types of debt can be considered "good debt" and other types are "bad debt." Most people believe having a little debt isn't all that bad. And a lot of people believe that some kinds of debt, such as student loans, are actually good. With the student loan crisis on the rise, I think it's pretty obvious that it has done more damage to this generation than it has helped it.

This is a lukewarm approach to debt. The mind-set of good debt versus bad debt allows people to justify their decision to go into debt. No matter how you slice it, there is no such thing as good debt and bad debt. It's just debt. At the end of the day, you still owe someone something, and those payments limit your options today and tomorrow.

The second mind-set—and possibly the most infuriating one—is that debt just isn't a big deal. In fact, people who buy into this thinking believe debt can help you get where you want to go. I've talked to far too many people who have been in this "debt isn't a big deal" mind-set for years. They go into debt not really thinking at all about the future, but in the present they feel like debt is the best solution for whatever they're facing. Their decisions include charging new TVs on credit cards or financing a new car because they want to make a good impression at work. They say things like, "We can totally afford this monthly payment for five years!" Even things that unexpectedly come up, like a roof repair, get charged because "It's the only option." They say, "No big deal. We'll just pay it off quickly."

Then the unthinkable happens. They lose their job. They get injured and are unable to work for six months. A huge emergency comes up and pushes their credit limit to the extreme. The bonus wasn't quite as big as they expected. By using debt to "help" them get what they wanted or needed, they bet on the future working out exactly as they planned. Only it didn't.

Things happen in life. And when we live with the mind-set that debt is somehow a good thing or is here to help us succeed in life, we live with the risk of that decision. These are lies—lies that are wrecking our lives.

Change Your Thinking

If we're going to change our habits around debt, we have to start by changing our thinking. And we can't change our thinking if we're not honest about what we believe and value. Many of us don't recognize the heavy influence our culture, friends, and family have on our thinking and behavior.

The bottom line is, it doesn't matter how much money you make; it matters how much you keep. Debt actually moves you backward in your financial life, enabling you to *spend* more than you *make*. Ask yourself this: Would you rather earn $45,000 a year or $450,000 a year? The answer seems obvious—until you bring up debt. A person making $45,000 a year who only spends $35,000 will build more wealth over time than the person making $450,000 and spending $475,000. In this situation the person with ten times more income is accumulating more and more debt every year, while the other person is slowly building lasting wealth. You can't earn your way out of debt unless you decide that debt is something you want to eliminate from your life once and for all.

THE SLIPPERY SLOPE

Debt never appears as a big scary monster at first. It slowly creeps into your life one decision at a time. But before you realize what's happening, debt is smothering you and keeping you from living your life on your terms and truly living a life you love. Let's take a look at how that slow crawl into debt happens at such a young age for so many people.

Off to a Bad Start

The world of debt for many people begins at age eighteen, with teens who are just starting to make adult decisions and who are barely old enough to vote. Our society has decided that you need to wait until you're twenty-one to buy alcohol and twenty-five to rent a car, but you can get a credit card and a student loan the day you turn eighteen.

The path of debt often starts on college campuses all across this country. Our culture tells you that you can't be a student without a student loan and that the idea of not going into debt for college is absurd. They want you to believe that if you don't go to college, you'll end up rejected and fighting off poverty, right? So the only way to avoid such a horrible fate is to aggressively apply for as much debt as you need to make college "affordable." It doesn't matter how much you take out because there will be a great job after you graduate that will give you the ability to pay it off easily. At least that's what most guidance counselors, college recruiters, and financial aid advisors tell you. I don't think for a second that these people *mean* to bring harm to students, though. I just think they've bought into the lie that student loans are a necessary evil for most students to go to college. And I disagree.

A Series of Wrong Turns

The pressure on parents is just as fierce. If a student can't get enough loan money for school, then their parents have the option to take out more. This isn't a smart move. But who wants to be the only parent whose child doesn't go to the best college, or any college at all? This is where the comparison game trips us up again.

So, with or without your parents' help, you do what any reasonable, logical, and rational person would do: you sign your name on the dotted line no matter what dollar amount is attached to that commitment. The reality of paying the loans back seems so far away that it doesn't even feel real. It's so far down the road that your time is better spent focusing on more pressing needs like what meal plan you should choose.

Then, often within the first few weeks of moving onto campus, you sign up for your first credit card. For just a few minutes of your time and a little personal information, you're approved for your very own card—and you get a free T-shirt or pizza as a bonus. Those credit card companies are so generous, aren't they?

You don't think it's that big of a deal. You just accept the fact that having a credit card is part of adulthood. Everyone is doing it, right? It can't be all that bad.

You decide to combine your newfound freedom at college (paid for with debt) to swipe your way through dinners, weekend parties, new clothes, and road trips. Then the bill comes in the mail—along with the startling reality that the part-time retail job you work in between classes won't cover the minimum payment. But don't worry. One quick call to a *different* credit card company and you can just move the whole balance onto another card. You end up playing a game with multiple card companies, always using one to pay off the other.

Paying the Piper

Shortly after graduation, you realize you need a new car to go along with that hard-earned degree you just received. You had your high school car. Then you had your college car. Now you need your grown-up car. Besides, it will help you land that high-paying job your college promised you would get by attending their school.

Of course, you can't buy a *used* car. They're not safe. Plus, used cars are junk. New is the only option. You need the $40,000, brand-new car to be taken seriously. New cars make the best impression, so that's what you decide to purchase.

So you visit another nice group of people who help you determine the monthly payment you can afford and show you what cars you can buy for that "low" monthly payment. This often happens before you even know your budget.

Once you have that nice, new car, you find a special someone, fall in love, and get married. You're married for about five minutes before people start telling you that you're throwing your money away renting and that you should buy a house. So you buy a house with practically nothing down (because you have practically nothing). Then that house needs a new roof and water heater within a year of you moving in.

Suddenly, you look up and realize that more than half of your family's income is going to debt payments and everything seems to be piling up. You don't really understand how you got there, but you know for certain that this is not the life you wanted. And the saddest part is that you have little to show for all the debt you're managing.

FACING YOUR MISTAKES

If this sounds familiar, if this is how your life has gone so far, I don't want you to feel shame or guilt for the choices you've made. I *do* want you to know there is a way out. You can live a life without debt, and you can make a habit to avoid it forever. It may seem crazy, but it's possible.

Don't get me wrong. I know that not every person is living with an overwhelming amount of debt. But debt has become so socially acceptable that's it's easy to think it's just a part of life. Few people in your life will ever challenge you on it either. That's where I come in. I'm not too worried about stepping on people's toes to talk about it.

We're going to take debt on, even if it fights back. We'll start by walking through the common types of debt. Then we'll learn how to steer clear of them from now on!

4

Dealing with Debt

I still think back on the night Winston and I went out on our first date. When the bill came, he paid for both of our meals. (Yes, he is a true gentleman.) But he did so with his credit card. Now listen, I'm not that crazy money chick who freaks out when other people's habits are different from mine. I never said anything about it on the date, but, given how I grew up, I did find it ironic that my date bought me dinner with a credit card.

As time went on and our relationship became more serious, I told him about my feelings toward debt of any kind. I wanted to steer clear of debt in every area of my life and in every way. Thankfully, he agreed and the credit card was history. So, from that point on in our relationship, we decided together to live without debt—and that even meant saying no to credit cards.

You may be thinking, *But, Rachel, having a credit card doesn't mean you have to go into debt. You can use a credit card wisely. Everybody knows that!* Well, here's where you may start to call me extreme. I don't think there's anything "wise" about credit cards at all. At the end of the month, you still *owe* MasterCard money. I am perfectly fine with someone calling me a radical when it comes to my stance on debt. I'm okay with being different on this topic. I never want to owe anyone anything. I want to use my money and that's it. Plain and simple. Because I believe the old saying is true: "If you play with snakes, you're going to get bit."

To steer clear of debt for life, we have to start thinking differently than what's considered "normal" in our culture. So let's start with my favorite debt topic, the one I get the most pushback on all the time. That's right. It's time to talk credit cards.

PLASTIC GENIES

One of my favorite things about my job is going to New York City to do morning talk shows like *Good Morning America*, *TODAY*, and *Fox & Friends*. Not too long ago, while I was there doing some interviews, I went to a Broadway show—the musical *Aladdin*. Anything with singing and dancing is my kind of show. In another life I'd no doubt be on a stage singing and dancing, either on Broadway or headlining my own world concert tour. But since I can't sing a note, I'll stick with helping people with their money.

During the first act, Aladdin finds the lamp, rubs it, and the genie appears. The genie gives Aladdin three wishes. He can ask for anything in the world he wants, but he only gets three wishes. In that moment it hit me. The genie's offer is kind of like a credit card. It gives you the chance to buy just about anything you want, just like magic. Except with credit cards, you feel like you get a lot more than three wishes. The only thing stopping you is the credit limit on your card.

But if you did rub a magic lamp and a credit card popped out to offer you three wishes, what would they be? Based on how people use their credit cards, I have some ideas.

Wish #1: I Want to Have What Everyone Else Has

This isn't surprising. Why? Because credit cards are so thoughtlessly "normal." Everyone has at least one, right? How many of your friends don't have credit cards? More than likely none. The credit industry wants nothing more than for you to believe that credit cards are just a way of life and that choosing not to have one means you are missing out on life. The message becomes, "If you want to be like everyone else, you need a credit card. No one uses cash anymore. Just swipe this card! It's so easy and convenient! Plus you get perks like cash back and airline miles!"

These messages sink in over time, slowly convincing people that they need a card not only to fit in but also to survive in the modern world. So, almost without giving it a second thought, they fill out the application and one, two, or twenty cards arrive in the mailbox almost overnight, ready for whatever purchases they can rack up.

Normal Is a Trap

If being normal is such a priority, let's take an honest look at what "normal" really means. The average household has more than $15,000 in credit card debt.[1] The average college graduate leaves school with around $35,000 in student loan debt.[2] The average car loan adds on another $28,000 in debt.[3] You add all that together, and it paints a pretty terrible picture of what's going on with the Joneses. I don't know about you, but that doesn't sound like a life I'd love.

In the last chapter we said that debt makes you a slave, and this is how. The average family in this country has absolutely no say in how a huge portion of their income is spent. They can't use that money to fund retirement, upgrade their home, take amazing family vacations, give it away to a cause they are passionate about, or do anything else because they have to send it out to their creditors every month. Throw in a mortgage, taxes, and the general cost of living, and the normal family has little to no margin in their lives at all.

Helping you become normal is not my goal for this book. I don't want you to be like everyone else and do what they're doing with their money. They're throwing it away! They're like a rat in a wheel, running as hard and fast as they can but going nowhere. I don't want that to be you. If that's your goal, then I'm afraid you picked up the wrong book. But if your goal is to take control of your money and live the life you *really* want to live, then saying good-bye to credit cards and "normal" thinking is the right direction.

The "Perks" Aren't Worth It

People tell me all the time that the main reason they choose to use a credit card over another form of payment is for all of the rewards they get. From cash back to airline miles, credit card companies have done a great job drilling this concept into our minds. "I am going to take my points and fly to Europe for free." I can't tell you how many times I have heard that line.

How many reward miles do you think *have never been used* by frequent flyers? Fourteen trillion![4] That's enough miles to fly to Pluto and back 2,000 times! That's how many unused miles people currently have. And so the thinking goes, *I am going to spend more money, because the more I put on the card, the more miles I will get for that trip to Europe.* That probably isn't going to happen. Thousands of people have the same intentions, but they never actually take that exciting trip.

Don't fall into this mind-set. Think about all the extra money you are spending just to get those points or airline miles. A credit card isn't an investment. The only thing you *earn* with a credit card is a lot of debt, stress, and worry. The interest you're paying out and the stress on your life aren't worth the perks, airline miles, T-shirts, and free pizzas the credit card company uses to hook you.

Wish #2: I Wish I Could Pay for Emergencies

One of the most common excuses I hear from people signing up for credit cards is, "Oh, I'll only use this for emergencies." These pieces of plastic have really become a false safety net for a lot of people. In fact, credit cards have become the go-to for people in a financial emergency. Car breaks down? Credit card. Home HVAC goes out? Credit card. Suddenly forget that Christmas is this month? Credit card. Okay, that last one isn't really an emergency, but I bet you know people who act like it is!

You know what else works great in an emergency? Cash. The only difference is that having cash set aside for emergencies requires a little time and discipline. It can be difficult to build this up, but if you make it a priority, it can happen. Having a solid emergency fund in the bank gives you the confidence to get rid of your credit cards for good. Too many people reach for their plastic when their car breaks down, but you know what that does? It turns a car problem into a money problem. But when you have actual money in the bank just for emergencies, you can simply get the car fixed. No stress, no drama.

An emergency fund will be your safety net when emergencies happen. It's hard to get *out* of debt if you keep going *into* debt because of emergencies, so putting some money in the bank is the first step. The inevitable is going to happen, so plan for it. The emergency fund will keep you from taking on more loans and putting stuff on a credit card. It will also give you peace of mind knowing you have cash on hand.

Here's what I recommend: begin with the starter emergency fund of $1,000. This will cover smaller emergencies while you're getting out of debt, which we will talk about a little later. Things like car troubles, small medical emergencies, and smaller house issues fall into this category. And if you have to dip into the emergency fund, just make sure you build it back up as quickly as possible.

Once you are out of debt, you should grow your emergency fund to a full three to six months of expenses. This is a long-term goal. Ironically, most people who have saved a full emergency fund generally try not to use it because it's their stable source of security. With no debt at that point, it's easier to cash flow little accidents and keep the emergency fund tucked away for the huge problems. This becomes the "new normal."

When you use debt in the face of a crisis, you're only making things worse. You're treating one problem by creating another. We'll talk a lot more about the emergency fund later. For now, just remember that a credit card makes a terrible emergency fund.

Wish #3: I Want to Buy Things As Conveniently As Possible

I know many people who use credit cards for literally every purchase they make, all day every day. From gas to groceries to dinner to a pack of gum, they'll flip that little piece of plastic onto the counter and spend money without even thinking about it. And they all say basically the same thing, "Hey, this is money I'd have to spend anyway. Why not make my life easier by putting all my expenses on this one card? I'll pay it off every month."

This may be true for some people but not most. In fact, the average American family who has at least one credit card carries an outstanding balance of $15,762.[5] So the truth is that saying, "I will pay mine off every month" is wishful thinking.

Even if they have the best intentions, something else always pops up and keeps them from paying the card off every month. Then the bill comes at the end of the month and they realize they don't have enough to cover it. So they make a payment and leave a balance on the card. Repeat that every month, and you've got a huge credit card debt sneaking up behind you.

The Credit Card Alternative

Honestly, it's hard to argue against the convenience factor of a credit card when you're standing at the cash register. Who wants to be checking out at the grocery store and counting out dimes and nickels to get exact change? It's so much easier to just swipe. I understand! That's why I swipe my debit card. A debit card will do everything a credit card will do *except* get you into debt.

Debit cards often get a bad rap. Many people think they aren't as safe as credit cards, but that simply isn't true. Visa debit cards, for example, have offered the same protection on their branded debit cards as they do on their credit cards for years. That's even spelled out on Visa's own website.[6] And new security features are making your debit card even safer. The newer debit cards that come with a computer chip on the card itself add more layers of protection to your debit transactions, making the store and the bank both liable for fraudulent charges. Rules around these protections are changing as the technology changes, so it's something you should check out with your bank.

Traveling on Debit, Not Credit

Did you know you can actually travel with just a debit card? I am surprised by the number of people who don't realize this. It's true. You can even check into a hotel and rent a car. The tradeoff is hotels and rental car companies will put a hold on your debit card. The range varies, but it's usually not an astronomical amount. Occasionally, a hotel or car rental place may try to charge you more or give you a hard time for using debit. If you find one of those places, I suggest you keep looking. You never want to base your financial plan on what's best for someone else.

Some people freak out and say they can't afford the hold because they don't have any extra money in their checking account. If you don't have a cushion in your checking account when you travel, or the ability to pull some from savings, you shouldn't be traveling and staying in a hotel in the first place. That might sound rather harsh, but if the hold on your debit card is going to stress you out financially, you may need to step back and take another look at your travel plans.

This is something Winston and I have to keep in mind when we travel. Part of our planning for trips is to remember there might be a hold on our debit card during the trip. We just plan around it. Some would say this is a major inconvenience, but it's simply a tradeoff we are willing to make. I would rather do this type of planning than worry about paying a credit card bill at the end of the month.

Cash Still Exists

Another alternative to the credit card is a little more old school—*cold, hard cash*. In fact, did you know you actually spend less when you use cash? Why? Because cash is emotional; you feel the transaction when you pay with tangible currency. A study by Carnegie Mellon found that your brain experiences a little emotional pain, because you actually understand that you are spending money—money that you worked hard for.[7] You don't get that same sensation when you swipe a piece of plastic, so you end up spending more on your purchases. A debit card is a little different because you know you are spending your money, but with a credit card there is little emotion attached to a purchase.

Plus, using cash is a great reminder that money is finite; it has limits. When it's gone, it's gone. But if you just go through your day swiping your credit card everywhere you go, it's easy to slip into the magic genie mentality. That's why I think it's a good idea to use cash for certain types of purchases, like for clothes, entertainment, or eating out. It's one of the easiest ways for me to keep track of how much I actually have to spend in those areas.

The Bottom Line

As much as I wish there were a magic genie that could make all of our financial dreams come true, that's not reality. The reality is that you can live the life you want, but the real magic is in your ability to handle money wisely. That means steering clear of debt—especially credit cards.

SAY GOOD-BYE TO STUDENT LOANS

As I walked off the stage after speaking at a conference in Phoenix, a woman was waiting for me. You could see she was deep in thought, maybe even a little stressed. After we introduced ourselves, she started opening up. I actually get this a lot. Within thirty seconds of meeting someone, they might tell me their name, how much money they make per year, and how much debt they have!

She told me that she met her husband at college, and they had gotten married after graduating nine years earlier. They both left college with student loan debt—a combined total of $80,000 to be exact. Not long after getting married, she enrolled in graduate school in order to become a college professor. Halfway through her master's program, she got pregnant with their first child. Surprise! To make a long story short, they now have two kids, two college degrees, half the classes needed to complete her master's program, and tens of thousands of dollars of debt to show for it.

She was at this conference because she wanted to find a way to stay at home with her kids. The sad reality, though, was that the math just didn't work. She has to keep working just to keep up with their student loan payments, and some of those payments are for a degree she doesn't even have. Now, instead of teaching college-level English, she's working as a receptionist at a dental office. Of course, that's a great job if you love what you're doing, but she doesn't. She'd rather be teaching or staying home with her kids. A dental office wasn't even on her radar when she was racking up all those student loans. And that's exactly what debt does. It steals your options. She doesn't want to be working at all right now, let alone in a job she's not passionate about, but she has no choice.

Breaking Up with Sallie Mae

If you have student loans—and, statistically speaking, it's pretty likely that you do—please don't take this story as condemnation from me. This is a judgment-free zone, I promise. But I want you to get to a point where you *hate* your student loans. I want you to get passionate about paying them off. Excusing your loans by saying, "It's no big deal" or "Everybody has them" keeps you in debt for a long time. In fact, I've talked to people in their fifties who are still paying for their degrees. Sallie Mae has been a part of their lives for so long they think she's a roommate. If that's you, it's time to kick her out of your house for good!

There is some confusion around what you can do with your big pile of student loan debt, so let's clear it up.

Bankruptcy Won't Help

The first thing you need to know, which a lot of people don't realize, is that bankruptcy won't free you from student loans. Even if you file for bankruptcy, your student loans will likely be unaffected. Current bankruptcy law exempts education loans unless doing so would cause the consumer undue hardship. But "undue hardship" isn't clearly defined, so each court decides, meaning there's a good chance you won't be able to get out of your student loans through bankruptcy.

You Can't Depend on a Hopeful Future Income

Many people also buy into the assumption that going into debt for any degree is worth it. People think, *I'll be able to pay this off when I get a job and earn a great income. Having a master's degree automatically means I will earn more money.* Unfortunately, that's not always the case. True, you *might* earn more, but you or your spouse *might* also end up wanting to stay home with the kids or do something else. You never know what will happen in the future, so you don't want to tie up your future by piling up a ton of debt.

Graduates often believe they'll make more money if they get a certain degree or go to a certain school, so they'll go deeply into student loan debt to make it happen. The problem is, that's often not the case. In fact, a recent survey from the Pew Research Center found that "households headed by a young, college-educated adult without any student debt obligations have about seven times the typical net worth ($67,000) of households headed by a young, college-educated adult with student loan debt ($8,700)."[8] Seven times the net worth! Why? It's because these students worked hard, made wise choices, went to the schools they could afford, and didn't graduate tens of thousands of dollars in the hole from student loans.

Student Loan Consolidation Isn't a Magic Bullet

I'm not a big fan of debt consolidation in general, but student loan consolidation can make a difference in your overall payoff goal. If you do choose to consolidate your student loans, make sure the new interest rate is lower overall than the interest rates of your current loans. Most of the time you can only consolidate them once, so watch the rates carefully and try to lock in the lowest rate possible.

My only word of caution: If you do consolidate multiple loans into a new single loan at a lower rate, it will seem like a much bigger mountain to climb when you start paying it off. If you keep them separate, you will feel the quick wins as you are paying off your debt, which is extremely motivating. It may make more sense financially to lump them together, but get ready for the emotional toll of looking at one big balance on your statement every month as you work to pay it all off.

The Best Way to Get Rid of Student Loans

If you do have student loans, my advice is to pay them off quickly. *Quickly* is the key word here. Don't settle for your minimum payments. Double, triple, or quadruple those payments and get Sallie Mae out of your life once and for all! Treat her like she is an ex-girlfriend. What if your ex moved in with you and started taking money out of your bank account every month? You'd kick her out, right? Do the same with Sallie Mae. And while that may feel overwhelming and impossible right now, just get comfortable hating your student loan. We'll give you a more comprehensive plan for getting out of debt later on.

THAT NEW CAR SMELL

I firmly believe that a car loan is the dumbest type of debt you could ever take on. If you simply look at the math, you are borrowing money and paying interest on something that is going down in value. To be clear, that means you're paying *more* for something that's worth *less* the instant you drive it off the lot—and you continue to lose money every month. Mathematically speaking, it's just not a smart idea.

The Cost of That Smell

I once tweeted, "The average car payment in America is $492. If you invested that every month for the next forty years, you would have $5,846,153! #paycash." You would have thought I ran over someone's puppy. People came out of the woodwork protesting and yelling at me (IN ALL CAPS) about how crazy I was to think someone could pay cash for a car. "You have no idea what it's like to live in the real world," one person said. "I like my Lexus, and I pay over $500 a month for it. I would rather have that than a junky car."

Thankfully, some people agree with me and tell me their stories of paying cash for cars. A friend at work recently told me that she bought a car that she had wanted for years—a beautiful, white Mercedes sedan. She had rented one almost ten years earlier, and that memory stuck with her all this time. When it was time to replace the car she was driving, she went on a hunt to find that very car. Imagine how excited she was to tell me that she found the exact car, in great condition, for only $6,000! Sure, it had some miles on it, but it looked amazing and was mechanically perfect. So now she's driving a like-new Mercedes that looks and drives as great as any other luxury car you'd see at a stoplight—and she paid cash for it!

But that's definitely not the norm in our culture. Most people you talk to think you will always have a car payment. If that is your mind-set, if the two cars in your driveway are stealing $1,000 in car payments from your hard-earned money every month, it will be hard for you to win with money.

Here Come the Buts

Every time I talk about cars, I immediately get pushback from people who are doing their best to justify a completely ridiculous car payment. Some of the most common "buts" I get are:

"But it's at 0% interest. Isn't that a great deal?"

No, it's not, because that new car starts losing money the instant you drive it off the lot. From the first month of ownership, you will owe more on your car than it's worth. Four years later, you'd still have a year or two of payments left on it, but your car would have lost around 60 percent or more of its value. Besides, zero percent is not the same as cash, and not everyone who falls for the zero percent marketing pitch actually qualifies for the deal. But, by then, they're already in love with the car of their dreams and are willing to sign anything to drive it home. And, of course, some of those "deals" aren't quite as attractive once you read the fine print. Listen, making money off of car loans is their business. You're not outsmarting anyone.

"But I just had a baby, so I need a safe car—like a new Tahoe."

This is one I hear all the time from people who are having kids. Do babies take up more room? Yes. Do you want your baby to be safe in the car? Yes. But those things don't equal a new Suburban. Safe doesn't mean new. There are plenty of safe, pre-owned cars out there for you to get a good deal on. You can't tell me a four-year-old Toyota 4Runner isn't safe.

I'm talking to myself on this one, by the way. I think the cool new SUVs are gorgeous! But I always have to stop, take a breath, and check my motivations for wanting one. Sometimes, I think I'm more drawn to the car as a status symbol than anything else. Maybe you are too. We can't let our desire to keep up with the Joneses drive our money habits and decisions, though. Remember, the Joneses are broke. Keeping up with broke people who are just trying to look rich is a bad plan.

"But how am I supposed to buy a car without a car loan?"

The answer is simple, but you may not like it: save up and pay cash for your cars. Yes, I'm serious. Hey, if you're like the average American, you're probably paying around $500 a month in car payments anyway. Why not just pay yourself that $500 a month for a year and buy yourself a $6,000 car? My friend got a beautiful Mercedes for that, remember? Drive it around while you keep saving, then sell it and upgrade again. All it takes is a new decision to pay *yourself* instead of the bank. If you have a car loan, go crazy and pay it off quickly or even sell it to get this process rolling on paying yourself instead of the bank!

The first car you buy with cash might not be your dream car, and that's okay! But just because it's not your dream car doesn't mean it has to be a junker. Buying used doesn't mean buying a crappy car. You can find a great used car. You can even find a nice, well-cared-for, ten-year-old Lexus or Infinity at a great price in pretty much any city in America. Pick out a car with a body style that doesn't change often. I can't tell you how many luxury brands I see on the road, and I have no idea what year they are. They could be brand-new or eight years old, and I wouldn't be able to tell just by looking at it. The moral of the story is this: own your cars; don't let them own you!

RELATIONSHIP-DAMAGING LOANS

Some of the most damaging debt people get into are loans to or from friends or family. It's sad how many relationships are strained or even ruined because of money. The stories I've heard from people who have lost decades-long friendships or broken family ties because of "friendly loans" are heartbreaking. It's always, *always* best to keep debt out of your relationships.

What Are Friends For?

I understand the intention behind loaning money to someone you love. A parent wants to help their grown child with college or a new car, so they loan them money, expecting them to pay it back. A woman loans her brother money to start a new business. A guy loans his friend money because he's in a tight spot. People in these situations often have the best intentions, but what are they really risking? First, they are risking that friend or family member never paying them back. Second, they risk losing the relationship because, almost always, stress and judgment start to seep in.

Here's what happens when you loan money to a friend or family member. You start looking at what they're doing more closely. You see them take a vacation, and you think, *They still owe us $3,000.* Then resentment sets in. Or if you *borrow* money from your brother and sister-in-law, suddenly Christmas with the whole family feels like you are sitting by the Christmas tree opening gifts . . . with your banker. You feel guilty, like you need to justify the fact that you've spent the $10,000 they gave you, still haven't found a job, and have no idea when that money will be paid back.

Sure, there are some situations where everything works out fine. But more often than not, people regret loaning or borrowing money, especially when it involves friends and family. It's just not worth putting your relationship at risk. Don't fool yourself here—your relationship will change. It will change from family or friend to the borrower and lender. The myth tells us that if we loan money to a friend or relative, we are *helping* them. The reality is that the relationship will end up either strained or destroyed. In fact, 57 percent of those polled have seen a friendship or relationship end because of loaned money, and 63 percent have seen people skip out of repaying a friend or family member.[9] Don't risk your relationships by throwing a loan into the mix.

I was talking about this with a friend recently, and she told me how she had loaned money several years ago to someone who was having financial trouble. She did this in a great spirit, truly wanting to help out her friend—a great guy who had just lost his job. He said he needed help, so my friend helped him. Sadly, what happened next changed their relationship forever. A few weeks later she was checking her Facebook feed and saw the guy's post that day: "Just bought the new iPad! Wow, this thing is awesome!" Can you imagine how annoying that would be? Again, everyone had great intentions, but she's never going to look at that person the same way again. In her mind, all she did was buy this guy an iPad instead of helping him pay rent and buy food, which was her intention.

Loaning Your Signature

While we're talking about loaning money, I want to say a word about cosigning too. That word is *no*. N-O. Don't do it! Cosigning seems a little more socially acceptable than flat-out loaning someone money, but it can actually put you in a much worse place financially. Cosigning usually comes into play for a car, house, or student loan. This is effectively the same thing as loaning the person actual money, except it has a bit of a surprise-party element to it. If your friend or family member defaults, it becomes your debt. But you never know if or when that day will come.

If the bank asks for a cosigner, it means they don't have confidence that the person who needs the loan will pay it back. Red flag! Seriously, if the bank—whose entire business is built around loaning money—doesn't think someone is good for a loan, they're probably right. They don't make judgment calls on whether your friend is a good person, and they don't care how sweet she may be. They just know she most likely won't pay them back, and when she doesn't, they'll come knocking at your door.

If you cosign, you're just as legally responsible for that debt as your friend, and, trust me, the bank will make sure they get their money. Do you think my friend was annoyed when she found out she basically bought someone an iPad? Well, just think how she'd feel if she had ended up buying someone a car!

So How Can You Help?

In many of these situations, the heart and motivation are almost always good, especially if these relationships seem solid. But loaning or cosigning seldom ends well. If you have the money and the heart to help, my advice would be to skip the loans and just give your friend or family member the money. That's right. Give it to them.

Give with the condition that it never has to be paid back and the clear understanding that it is not a loan. But only give if you can afford it, have the cash available, and there are no strings attached. You have to be in a place where you can emotionally let go of that money and know whatever they decide to do with the cash is up to them.

It's important to remember, though, that there is a difference between helping and enabling. You always have the option to say no. *No* is a complete sentence. If you are in a situation where you know you shouldn't give someone money because he or she will not be wise with it, you don't have to give them the money. You don't want to enable any bad money habits, putting that person in a worse situation than they were in to begin with. You can say no and walk away. That might seem harsh, but you are *helping* them by saying no. If you just keep handing them money, you are causing them more harm than good.

DEBT IS A (BAD) CHOICE

This is your life, and you must make up your own mind. How are you going to live it? Are you going to be tied down to credit card bills and student loans for the next fifty years? Or are you going to say you are done paying out your hard-earned money to the bank? To move forward, you have to have a clear sense of what you think and believe about debt. This may mean exchanging your "depending on debt all the time" habit for a "steering clear of debt" habit.

Winston and I make this choice every day. And we decide to

steer clear of debt intentionally. We're never going there, and you don't have to either. It's time for you to get rid of whatever debt is in your life—and this time for good. Ready? Then let's take a look at what a debt-free life really looks like!

5

A Life without Debt

Imagine for a moment that you had no payments. Zero payments. You owe nothing. Just let this sink in for a bit. The fifteenth and thirtieth of each month come around, you receive your paycheck, and that's it. You don't have to pay a single credit card bill. That $500 car loan is now $500 you get to keep. And Sallie Mae who? Do you feel the freedom? Do you feel a weight lifted off your shoulders? Does your stress level lower?

Let's go a step further. Think about how empowering it would be if you got even more radical and paid off your house in seven years versus thirty years. What if you invested your house payment at the age of thirty-five instead of sending it to the bank? What would retirement look like for you? What if this were your life? Where could you go? What could you do? How much more could you save? How much more could you invest? How much more could you give? It's pretty amazing to think about, isn't it?

This dream of having no payments is the mind-set I need you to be in as we look into a life of getting out of debt and steering clear of it forever. The best news of all is it doesn't have to be just a dream in your imagination. This can be your reality.

CHOICES AND TRADE-OFFS

In order to make steering clear of debt a habit in your life, you have to really want that for yourself and your family. It's always seemed interesting to me that some people are willing to change their habits in just about every other area of their lives except money. They're willing to follow a diet plan, train for a marathon, or even hire a personal trainer. Because these things are important to them, they organize their lives around doing them. So why is it so hard to steer clear of debt?

I believe most people fail to steer clear of debt because they simply don't believe they can live a life without debt. They don't see how they can make that kind of drastic change in their lives at this point. You see, if you have credit cards, car loans, or student loans, debt was a choice you made at some point in your life. It's not fun, sexy, or immediately gratifying to kick debt out of your life. In fact, this decision will require a lot of work for a short period of time. And unless you're facing a true financial crisis, you likely don't have a sense of urgency around getting rid of it for good.

But if using debt was a choice you made at some point, you can make a new choice today. You can choose to steer clear of it from now on. If you're going to develop the money habits you need to live the life of your dreams, this is a choice you need to make right now. You *can* live without debt, and I want to show you how.

Go Ahead; Start an Avalanche

We've come to my favorite part of the no-debt habit—paying off your debt! I wish I had confetti to throw in the air because this is an exciting part of your journey. We have talked so much about the burden of debt and how annoying all those payments are, but now we get to eliminate them for good. Let's talk about how to do it.

Once you have the $1,000 starter emergency fund in place, it's time to get rid of your debt once and for all. The best way to get out of debt is to use what we call the debt snowball. This is where you list all of your debts, except your house, smallest to largest *by balance, not interest rate*. Pay the minimum payments on everything else and pay off the smallest debt first. You have to get mad at this debt! Take as much money as you can and throw it at the smallest debt on the list. Once that is paid off, take what you were paying on that one and roll it to the second smallest debt and so on and so on until you are debt-free! This is the most effective way to pay off debt because it addresses *behavior*.

You see, money isn't all about math and interest rates; it's also about your behavior. So, by paying off the smallest debt first, you get a quick win. And we all love that, don't we? Even if it is a $300 debt on a department store credit card, put it on the list and pay it off. When you're done with it, cross it off the list and move on to the next one. Quick wins help you stay motivated throughout this process and get you ready for the challenge of paying off bigger debts.

Go crazy when you're paying off debt. We're going to talk about how to have nice things in the near future (and even nicer things later)—but if you have debt, your first goal has to be getting free of that burden. That means making some short-term sacrifices for your long-term good. You might even consider getting an extra job for a few months. You may not go out to eat. You may say good-bye to cable. You may cut your lifestyle down significantly, but the more you can sacrifice and the more money you can put toward your debt right now, the faster you will be completely free to live the life of your dreams.

Remember, these sacrifices are only temporary. You won't have to live like this forever, and I *don't want* you to live like this forever. I'm on your side! I want you to live the life you want, but, in order to do that, you may have to make these kinds of sacrifices in order to take control of your money. The encouraging part of this is that the average family we work with who uses the debt snowball pays off all their debt in anywhere from eighteen to twenty-four months! That means you can be debt-free in just a year and a half to two years!

If you're facing a mountain of debt, and if you've settled into the mind-set that you'll *always* be in debt, you may not believe that you can be debt-free in less than two years. And honestly, depending on your debt and your income, it might take you longer than that. Or, believe it or not, it might take you a lot less time. I've seen families get serious about the debt snowball and pay off everything in half the time they expected! Why? Because they get so excited about each payoff that they'll do almost anything to add more money to their get-out-of-debt plan.

Plus, once you start the debt snowball rolling, it picks up more and more snow the faster it rolls! That's because every time you pay off one debt, you free up more of your income. That leaves you more money to throw at the next debt on the list.

Everyone's journey is going to look different. Some take longer than average, and others take just a few months. Either way, the best news of all is that it's possible. You *can* become debt-free. Do you feel it in your bones? I hope so!

Choose Your Trade-offs

I want you to go into your new, debt-free life with your eyes open, so let's be honest about something up front. Yes, you can choose a life without debt, but that decision will cost you something in the short term. Where there are choices, there are also trade-offs. Because of my decision to live without debt, I have to accept some inconveniences. When you live debt-free, you are trading the short-term rush of immediate gratification for the peace of financial success over the long term. And, honestly, that's not a choice many people are willing to make. However, as you make steering clear of debt more and more of a habit in your life, the value of all of these little trade-offs starts to become crystal clear.

Without a credit card, you won't have the false safety net of an emergency fund. That's why it's crucial to get your $1,000 emergency fund in place quickly. But when you have a full emergency fund, you get the peace that comes with simply writing a check to cover unexpected expenses instead of having to go deeper in debt during an already stressful time.

As we mentioned before, when you choose to live without a credit card and you travel, your debit card will have a hold on it from rental car companies and hotels, so you have to plan for that. In return, you get to enjoy your vacations without worrying about a mailbox full of bills waiting for you when you get home.

When you go to buy a new car, you won't even consider a car loan. Sure, you may not be able to buy the same kind of car with cash as you could buy on payments, but that's also the benefit: you won't have a car payment!

When your child begins to think about college, you will have to spend a lot of time researching colleges you can afford, and your child will begin applying for scholarships. And don't freak out, but your child may need to spend some time looking for a job to help pay the tuition. The benefits here are obvious: Your son or daughter will get a great education and get out of school without the tens of thousands of dollars of debt that their classmates will have. And you'll set your kids up to win in their own lives, passing on a great legacy of financial responsibility to the next generation.

These are just a few examples of some of the inconveniences your new debt-free habit will cause, but I hope you're starting to see how worth it they are!

Delayed Gratification

A life without debt also requires you to become patient. Giving in to the sudden impulse to buy whatever you want, whenever you want, is no longer an option for you. It is hard to say no to yourself sometimes—I'll be the first to admit how difficult that is. There are a lot of things I want *right this second*. But I either don't have the money or it wouldn't be wise for me to spend money on those things. So I simply don't buy them.

There's a reason people say patience is a virtue. Patience allows you to practice delayed gratification—to stop and work hard for something you want. In our world of instant satisfaction by debt, you can basically buy anything you want right when you want it. I think that convenience impacts not only our purchasing habits, but also other areas of our lives. It makes us less patient when we have to wait for other things, like a long-awaited vacation or even a simple doctor's appointment. Debt feeds our impatience on many levels, but when you introduce financial patience and discipline into your life, you'll be amazed at how other parts of your life seem to relax as well.

CREDIT SCORES

One of the biggest questions I get when I talk about debt-free living is about what happens to your credit score when you don't have debt. But before we get there, you first need to understand what a credit score is. This term is thrown out there all the time, and there are so many misconceptions around it.

What a Credit Score Really Indicates

A credit score is a number that companies use to measure an individual's credit risk. Very exciting, I know. Your credit score is calculated like this: 35 percent debt payment history, 30 percent debt amount owed, 15 percent length of debt history, 10 percent types of debt used, and 10 percent new debt. Do you see a theme here? It's all about *debt*. Your credit score is based on how well you interact with debt. It is not an indication that you're winning financially; it's just an indication that you have and use debt—perhaps a lot.

Just so we're clear: You could inherit $1 million today and your credit score wouldn't change a bit. A high credit score doesn't mean you're good with money or that you have a lot of money. It just shows that debt is a big part of your financial life. And all the pressure around credit scores creates a financial death spiral for a lot of people. They hear early on that they need to establish good credit, so they take out a loan and get a credit card. That makes their credit score go up, which enables them to go deeper into debt. The more debt they have and use, the more opportunities they have to go even deeper.

That's how people end up with a great credit score but hopelessly stuck in debt they may never repay. Does that sound like winning? I don't think so. Here's a helpful clue—if your credit score is higher than your bank account balance, you're headed in the wrong direction!

Low Score or No Score?

One thing you need to know as you steer clear of debt is that your credit score will go down over time. This is because you have stopped interacting with debt. Don't panic. This is a good thing. It seems countercultural, I know. It will take time for your credit score to go to "undetermined," which is a neutral state. At some point after years of not using debt at all, your credit score could actually just disappear!

By the way, that is what my credit score shows when I pull it up: undetermined. That means I don't have a credit score! And I have rented an apartment, pay for utilities, and have great insurance rates. A few of those things have required a little extra work, but so what? Remember the whole trade-off idea? Well this is a trade-off, but it's worth not having a credit score and having to do a little extra work than to deal with credit cards and loans just to keep a credit score. There are ways to get around in this life without a credit score. I personally have never had an issue not having a credit score. You never know how far cash can take you until you give it a try.

The Biggest Credit Score Headache

The biggest pushback I get on this topic, though, is with home buying. Now, a mortgage is the one type of debt I will not yell at you for (if you buy your home the right way, which we'll talk about later). But here's the deal: When you buy a home, a mortgage lender normally pulls your credit score as part of the application and evaluation process. If you have a good score, they will give you the loan. If you have a bad score, you won't get the loan. Thought-provoking stuff, I know.

But you can still get a mortgage even if you don't have a credit score. You need to qualify for what's called *manual underwriting*. This means an actual human being will look at your ability to repay a loan. Some mortgage companies will call this a "No Credit Score" or a "Non-Traditional Credit" process. Usually, for a conventional mortgage, you'll need a solid twelve-month mortgage or rental payment history and a few other records like utility, insurance, medical payments, or school tuition. You need to be current on a job for two years and current on all of your bills, like your cell phone and insurance. This hassle is obviously a trade-off to living debt-free. Because debt isn't a part of your life, you have freedom and peace, but that means you will have to do some extra heavy lifting for a time while getting qualified for a mortgage.

The qualifications do change, so you need to call around and do your due diligence to make sure you have all the information you need to be underwritten for a mortgage. This process will take some time. Again, because you don't have a number for the bank to look at, they have to actually look at you as a person. It might seem crazy to think that a bank *doesn't usually* take the time to look at a person's employment and bill-paying habits over a period of time before loaning them $300,000, but it's true. It's just easier for them to look at a number on a screen and make their decision. Too bad for them, making the bank's job easier isn't one of my financial priorities.

SAY NO SO YOU CAN SAY YES

Now those trade-offs aren't too bad, are they? I would say whatever you have to give up to live without debt is worth the peace of mind you'll have and the money you get to keep instead of sending it to the bank. The only person who gets rich when you go into debt is the bank. Period.

As you start getting out of debt, all your short-term sacrifices will be worth it. Imagine being completely debt-free, including your house, by the time you're forty-five years old! Your paycheck comes in and you get to decide what to do with it. You can pay for a vacation outright. Maybe you even save up and buy a second home! What you get back in your life when you are debt-free is margin. The margin of time, money, and emotion. It's amazing. True freedom is getting to live the life you want to live, along with living out your values, desires, passions, and dreams.

Getting out of debt goes against every message our culture tells us. Culture says, "Buy now. Pay later. Do what makes you happy in the moment, and don't worry about the future." We are told instant gratification is a good thing because it allows you to live the life you want to live right this second, even if you don't have the money to support it.

The problem with that way of thinking is that it will catch up with you—either in an unexpected way or just over time as it wears you down. *Be different.* Debt doesn't have to be part of your life. You can make a choice today to live differently. You can choose a life of freedom and peace while you live life on your terms and not Visa's.

To get to this place, you must live on less than you make and choose to live wisely and within your means. I know there are going to be temptations along the way. You may even fall back into bad habits with money again. We're all human. No one is perfect.

I know you can live this way because I have heard countless stories of people all across the country doing it. And I have been able to do it. For Winston and me, it's meant making decisions about our money ahead of time. Sometimes it's hard—hard to see all your friends go on vacation, hard not to get the furniture you really want before the party you're hosting, hard to turn down a dinner invitation because it's not in the budget (and instead offer to cook at your house). Those choices aren't fun in the moment, but they lead to an abundant life.

Winston and I still have to say no at times. But we say no a lot less often than we did when we were first starting out on our financial journey. When we didn't have money in the budget at the end of the month to go out to eat, we made the decisions necessary to bridge the gap until the next paycheck. In other words, we got creative. Now, we are able to say yes to those dinner invitations more often, because of what a debt-free lifestyle has enabled us to do—keep our paychecks.

Even if there is a mountain of debt between you and me, know that I am cheering for you at the top of my lungs on the other side to keep at it. Keep climbing. Don't stop working hard to pay off debt. You can do it. Keep going. It's possible.

When you eventually eliminate your debt, you'll get your life back. And nothing you can buy will ever make you feel as great as that.

Make a Plan for Your Money

6

Permission to Spend

Winston and I love to travel together. Getting away is one of our favorite things to do. A few years ago I had just come off an intense live-event season, and Winston was busier than ever with his work. We wanted to start a family soon, so we planned to take one last big vacation while it was still just the two of us. We decided to go to our number-one relaxation destination—the beach!

When we were on the plane heading to Florida, Winston leaned over and said, "Rachel, it's been a crazy travel season for you. I want you to relax and not worry about the budget on this trip. We both know what our budget is for the overall vacation, but I want you to just spend money and not worry. I will keep up with the budget. If we get close to our limit, I'll tell you and we can back off. But for now, just enjoy yourself and don't worry about money."

I looked at him and said, "Babe, you're telling me I don't have to think about the budget and can just spend money?" He nodded.

I couldn't have been happier in that moment. I told him he was letting me live in one of my greatest strengths—my spiritual gift of spending money! For the next few days, I was going to get to live it out. I was so excited!

A few hours later we were sitting by an amazing pool overlooking the beach. The setting was like something out of a magazine. A server walked by, and I asked her if they had chips and guacamole. "Yes," she replied. So I asked her to bring me an order, not even thinking about the price. All seemed right in the world. I was sitting by the pool with my husband, soaking in the sun. I had my favorite food—chips and guac—on the way. And I didn't have to worry about a budget—or so I thought.

When the food came, it was delicious but it made me thirsty. So I grabbed a menu to look at the drinks. Only then did I notice the price next to the chips and guacamole—$23. I almost choked. Did the avocados fall from heaven? The Mexican restaurant down the street from my house charges $4 for the same thing!

I tried not to let it rattle me, so I pushed through the discomfort and looked at the drinks. I wanted one of those frozen, fruity concoctions, but there was nothing on the menu for less than $20. The same server came by to see what I wanted, and I remember giving myself the old pep talk I hadn't heard in a while, *Rachel, spend the money. You're a spender. Do it. This is what you're good at.*

I opened my mouth to place my order, but I had a hard time spitting out the words. I couldn't stop thinking about how much everything cost. Then the drink arrived. Each time I took a sip, I couldn't help but think, *That was a dollar. That was another dollar.* I realized that there was no way to enjoy my budget-free self any longer. I so badly wanted to enjoy living without a budget for a few days and just spend without thinking about it, but I couldn't. The budget habit had become too deeply ingrained in me.

I looked over at Winston sitting next to me at the pool and told him I couldn't do it any longer. I didn't know if I was spending too much now, which might mean I may not be able to order an appetizer at dinner that night. He laughed. Then we sat by the pool budgeting out each meal of the trip. Once we did that, I knew I could order and enjoy what came without any stress or anxiety.

MONEY AND EMOTIONS

You have to understand that I love spending money. Love it. Probably more than I should. I'm not sure which I love more: the thrill of the hunt or the transaction process. Maybe a little of both. Either way, I'm a woman on a mission when I have cash, a plan, and something I need to buy.

So I am the first person to admit that having and following a budget is a challenge. Even the word *budget* sounds so restricting, boring, and dull. We really need to find a better word. Until then, *budget* will have to do.

Budget Misconceptions

I used to believe that living on a budget would mean I would never get to go out to eat, go shopping, or take vacations. I'd have to sit at home and hunt for coupons the rest of my life. In my mind, living on a budget meant not living life at all. I'd rather buy the brand I want and not have to settle for a cheaper one. I would rather live my life and enjoy it instead of setting aside every want and desire so I could live within the parameters of some budget.

I grew up understanding the need for and value of budgeting, but it didn't come naturally to me. The worst part of anticipating a budget was all the little details. There just seemed to be so much to keep up with in order to be successful. The whole thing had the potential to stress me out. I viewed the budget as a straightjacket, forcing me to be extremely organized all the time, and that's not how I'm wired.

Rewiring

Growing up, I realized that I wasn't a "detail person" from having to share a bathroom with my older sister, Denise. Her side of the bathroom was always perfect in every way. Everything was organized and color coordinated. Her toothbrush, cotton balls, face wash, and anything she was going to use that day was laid out on the counter in the order of their application. When you opened the drawer, her headbands and scrunchies (thank you, 90's fashion) were matched according to color. Even her hairdryer cord was wrapped perfectly around the handle. Her half of the bathroom looked like something you'd see in one of those "15 Ways to Organize Your Life" articles.

My side of the sink? To say it was the complete opposite would be an understatement. There was toothpaste everywhere. The cord of my hairdryer was so tangled that it was effectively six inches long. I had to stand up against the wall and bend over a little bit because the dryer wouldn't reach the top of my head! There was always a film of hairspray on my side of the counter, so it felt sticky and gross. Makeup was spilled everywhere. Looking back, it was actually really disgusting. Of course, I could easily find whatever I needed in an instant. But no one in my family appreciated my preference for convenience over tidiness.

And our closets? Denise's closet was so well-organized that when I borrowed her clothes (usually without asking), she would notice something was out of place the second she opened the door. As a result, another argument would break out. My closet? Well, that was like opening the door to a black hole. You were afraid to dig in too far because you might get lost forever. When it came to organization, I simply had a lot to learn.

Setting Aside Childish Things

As I've gotten older, I've come to grips with the reality that I have no choice but to become more organized and pay attention to details. My life, like yours, has a lot of moving parts, so being on top of details is crucial. While my closet and bathroom sink are still works in progress, I've certainly grown in this area of my life.

I still have to deal with all this "hardwiring" when it comes to living on a budget. Thanks to my parents, though, I eventually had all the tools I needed to create and live on a budget that fits my personality type. No excuses.

Mom and Dad gave each of us our own checking accounts when we turned fifteen. Every month, they would figure out how much they'd need to spend on our clothes, sports fees, and other normal teenage expenses, and they'd deposit that money into our accounts instead of paying for each thing individually. That meant we had to keep up with the money and pay for those things ourselves. If we ran out of money, we knew Mom and Dad would never bail us out. We either had to push through the month broke or find a way to make some extra money. After a couple of really bumpy months, spending way too much way too fast, I realized I had to get a handle on things. I needed some control, some guardrails, for how, when, and where I was going to spend my money. Enter the budget.

From age fifteen I've had a love–hate relationship with the budget. I love what it does and what it enables me to do. I love that it makes my money go further. I love that it sets me and Winston up to win today, tomorrow, and over the long haul. But sometimes I hate doing it. There, I admit it. Dave Ramsey's daughter doesn't always love doing a budget. I hate having to sit down and think of every little thing I may need to spend money on a month in advance. It hurts having to tell Future Me no to purchases I think I'll want to make later.

But over time budgeting hasn't just gotten *bearable*; it's become *enjoyable*. Crazy, right? I've had to get over a lot of emotional obstacles to doing a budget over the years, and now I want to help you do the same.

FREEDOM AND RESPONSIBILITY

As I took a good look at my resistance to living on a budget, I had to face a tough truth—it came down to me not wanting to grow up and be accountable. One thing we're supposed to learn as we transition into adulthood is that with freedom comes responsibility. In fact, every freedom is balanced by an equal amount of responsibility. You can't drive a car without following the road signs. You can't fill a pantry without having a job that pays for those groceries. You can't be physically fit without committing to a consistent workout schedule.

Somewhere along the way, many of us have convinced ourselves that it's okay to do whatever makes us happy in the moment without considering the impact our decisions will have on our futures. When people live like this, they upset the balance that exists between freedom and responsibility. Our unwillingness to grow up in some areas, like how we use money, will only force us to live life on someone else's terms and not our own. Being an adult isn't all fun and games. If you've been an adult for longer than twenty minutes, you know this well.

Freedom doesn't exist outside of responsibility. If we want to live life on our own terms, then we have to acknowledge there are certain boundaries we need to determine for ourselves—and then we must live within those guidelines. If we want *to take control of our money* instead of *having our money take control of us*, then we have to learn to live within a budget.

84

Plan for Your Money

I often hear a common theme when it comes to life and money. People tell me, "I just want to enjoy my money and trust that everything will work out without me having to worry about every little dime I spend." Most people don't want to feel like they're living out of control, but they fear that living on a budget will mean having no life at all. Working through that kind of thinking can be hard.

Is there an easy solution? Yes. But spenders like me won't be ready for that solution until we've identified and addressed the real problem: namely, that our wants, desires, and lifestyles can sometimes outpace our means. Our natural inclination is to want what we want, when we want it, and on our terms.

When we were babies, we were at the center of the universe. If we needed something, all we had to do was cry, laugh, or make cute noises, and someone would be there to take care of what we wanted. As we get older, we're supposed to move away from the idea that the world revolves around us and our needs. However, some people have never crossed that bridge. They continue to live as if they *need* whatever they desire at the moment, and they act as if whatever *thing* they want is essential for life itself. This is rarely the case.

People often tell me, "I make good money, but I have no clue where it goes." That reminds me of a John Maxwell quote. He says, "A budget is simply telling your money where to go instead of wondering where it went." How often do people get to the end of the month and honestly wonder where their money went? They feel completely out of control and like they have absolutely no margin in their lives. They pay the bills, but there doesn't seem to be a lot left over to enjoy or use however they want. It is defeating for them to know they make decent money but still feel broke.

I hear these kinds of things all the time:

"Rachel, how can I shop for groceries and buy organic products *on a budget?*"

"How can I take a great vacation *on a budget?*"

"How can I buy some new clothes for the new spring season *on a budget?*"

"How can I throw a creative birthday party for my son *on a budget?*"

Those are great questions that show a desire to live a great life but still be responsible with money. However, the problem lies deeper than what appears on the surface. As I dig down into the details of each person's situation, what I often find is they are asking a completely different question. They want to know, *"How can I do everything I want to do without having to make any sacrifices?"*

This is the challenge. Until we accept the reality that the freedom money brings also comes with the responsibility to manage it well, we'll never get to pursue the life we truly want. Instead, we'll always be playing catch-up with our random desires and whims. The unwillingness to say no to yourself is a terrible way to live. There is no magic formula here. Until you have a budget, you won't know how much you can spend—and you won't know when to tell yourself no.

It's that simple.

Wanting the Best

I'm on your team when it comes to wanting you to live a great life. I want you to be able to go out to great dinners with your spouse or friends. I want you to throw a cute birthday party for your son. I want you to go play a round of golf.

I wish I could wave a financial wand that would give you permission to do anything you wanted to do without worry, guilt, or responsibility.

But I can't.

And, seriously, I still struggle with saying no to myself sometimes. Most of us do. When you see something you want, even something small and insignificant, it never feels good to say no. When Winston and I were preparing for our first child, we went to register at a few different stores. Who knew how much baby gear is out there? It's unbelievable how much stuff you can buy for a seven-pound human being who can't even roll over yet. On top of that, it doesn't help that so much of it is downright adorable.

I had to resist the urge to buy or register for every cute thing I laid my eyes on. The biggest flare-up came when Winston and I walked through the doors of Pottery Barn Kids. Everything in the store was so charming. I felt like I had to have it all. Part of my brain just shut down, time stopped, and I immediately fell in love with just about everything I picked up.

I had often heard people say, "I just want the best for my kids." I would think, *Well, sometimes that means saying no to them and not giving them everything they want.* Now it was my turn. My daughter wasn't even born yet, and I had convinced myself in less than two seconds that she needed the best of everything!

One of those items was an adorable washcloth set. That's right. Washcloths. So after my baby showers had come and gone, I picked up a set of these white washcloths with a lavender, plaid border. I was so pleased with myself that I found the most precious washcloths in the world for the most precious baby in the world. No new-mom syndrome here—I was thinking with pure logic. Obviously.

I told Winston how I needed to order at least two more sets. He thought I was crazy. In his pragmatic, practical point of view, he reminded me that I could buy functional washcloths anywhere for half the price. In fact, we didn't need baby washcloths at all—we had a whole linen closet full of them!

Even so, the idea of saying no to these washcloths was physically painful for me. Now, could we afford to buy these washcloths? Yes. But because we set a baby budget, there was no room for that item which, honestly, was pretty unnecessary. The damage to the budget would be minimal, but it wasn't the most effective use of what we had set aside.

The same is true for everyday things like food. Going to the grocery store and sticking to a list and a specific spending amount can be tough. You may want to buy organic fruit and juice pouches for the kids. The idea of having a limit on what you can and cannot spend can be difficult to manage when you're running through the store after work, trying to make it home in time to prepare dinner. Sometimes it feels like there's no time for sticking to a budget.

But here's a different perspective. Instead of looking at a budget as confining, look at it as *permission to spend*. After living on a budget for years now, it's hard to imagine getting along without it. Even when Winston told me at the beach that I didn't have to think about the budget, my first thought was, *Freedom, here I come!* But then the habit kicked in.

I realized something through that experience. Living on a budget isn't constrictive or confining; it's just the opposite. It's the only way to live with any freedom. A budget helps me to enjoy my money more because I am in control of what I am spending. A budget is not a straitjacket. It's not a killjoy. A budget helps me live the life I want to live and do the things I truly value.

What a Budget Isn't

A budget is more than just keeping up with the bills. Some people who think they are living on a budget really just mean they pay what they owe every month and get by. They aren't living with an intentional plan. The bills come in, they pay them, and they hope there is money left over.

A budget isn't trying to create space on your maxed-out credit cards. The idea that living on a budget means staying within your credit limit is delusional. Paying off your credit card bill every month does not mean you are sticking to a budget.

In this mind-set you're just swiping at every opportunity that presents itself and then paying off the consequences at the end of the month. Using credit cards is like living your life through a rear-view mirror. A huge chunk of your paycheck covers food you have already eaten, movies you have already seen, and clothes you have already bought. You are living your financial life in the past instead of telling your money where to go for the future.

Where You Want to Go

A budget gives you the permission to spend your money in ways that will take you where you want to go. A budget means you can actually spend money on stuff you want. The purpose of a budget is not to *limit* your freedom but to *give* you freedom—with some boundaries in place.

It's amazing how a plan will free you up to love your life instead of making you feel like you're always running to catch up. When you plan this way, you're able to look at the future and gauge your life more effectively—instead of just spending money throughout the month not knowing where it's going.

People who live on purpose in any area of their lives, including money, are the people who not only win but thrive. People who have great marriages work hard on having a great relationship. They may read books, go to counseling, and have date nights. People who are healthy and in shape work out and eat right. People who are great parents listen to good child-rearing advice, read books on

89

discipline, talk to other moms and dads, and cultivate great relationships with their kids.

So people who win in life have to work hard and be intentional. The same is true when you're talking about your money. To win with money means you must make money work for you. That's what a budget is all about. Money doesn't just drift into your savings account. Debt doesn't get paid off on its own. You have to be purposeful and take control of it. You have to tell your money what you want it to do.

GIVING YOURSELF A RAISE

Many people have told me that when they started living on a budget, it felt like they got a raise. It's amazing how much money we can spend throughout the month on things that don't really matter. Ten dollars here and five dollars there can really add up. But when you sit down and are intentional with every dollar you have, every dollar will stretch further. That means you get to do more of the stuff you want to do and plan for the things you'll do in the future.

You can change your mind-set, your habits, and your life. Freedom and responsibility go hand in hand. You don't get one without the other. That means you can't live life on your terms and not pay attention to how you use your money. If you want to create good money habits, you must be willing to do whatever it takes, even if it's uncomfortable in the beginning. As you do, you'll find you can do more with your money than you ever thought possible.

Now that you know a budget is an important and crucial money habit, let's talk about how to actually build one.

7

Tell Your Money What to Do

One of my friends decided she was going to run a marathon. She's one of the most disciplined people I know, so it wasn't a complete surprise. Personally, I have no idea why anyone would want to run unless they're being chased by someone or something. For my friend, though, running was something she enjoyed. She was excited about the challenge of getting ready for the longest distance she had ever run.

My friend is also a planner. She did her research about running marathons as she was getting started. I couldn't tell you the number of different marathon running schedules she downloaded and reviewed. She read books, read blogs, and talked to people she knew who had done it before.

One of the secrets she discovered was that you have to decide everything in advance. She needed to know what days she was going to run and what days she was going to cross-train. She even needed to know what days she needed to rest and not do anything at all.

Once she worked out her training schedule, she knew everything she had to do, every day of every week, leading up to her race. One of her mentors explained that this is important because it would keep her from getting confused by her body and the voices in her head. She knew she wasn't always going to wake up and feel like doing the scheduled activity for the day. But if she checked every box as she had designed it, then she would have done everything to prepare for her first marathon.

I was so proud of her. She ran the race in the time she had predicted. And, since then, she's run many other marathons in the same way. It works for her. She didn't do anything that others hadn't done before; she simply wrote out a plan and then worked the plan by implementing the details.

This kind of planning works with running marathons, and it also works with managing your money.

GETTING STARTED

A budget's primary job—its only job, really—is to tell your money where to go. That's actually a biblical principle: "Suppose one of you wants to build a tower. Won't you first sit down and estimate the cost to see if you have enough money to complete it?" (Luke 14:28). No one ends up a millionaire by accident. You can accidentally *lose* a lot of money, but you don't keep, build, and multiply dollars by drifting into it. That has to be done on purpose.

It's probably safe to say that, at some point, you received money from a paycheck, a gift, or a tax return—and when you looked up a few weeks later, the money seemed to have just disappeared! That's a frustrating experience, especially when it's money you've worked hard for. You put in long, hard hours to earn that money, but have nothing to show for it thirty days later.

It's time to tell your money where to go. It's time to change the outcome of your life by developing new habits. One of those habits has to be building and living on a budget. Not only is this important when you're getting started, but it also becomes even more important as you begin to make more money.

Getting started is easier than you might think.

Timing Is Everything

The first principle to getting started is learning *when* to do a budget. A budget isn't just tracking expenses throughout the month. It's being intentional with your money *ahead of time*. So you'll need to do a budget before the month begins. That means planning ahead for what is going to happen. This is a simple yet important part of budgeting. The goal is to be *proactive* with your money rather than *reactive*.

You need to create a new budget every month. And you'll have to keep modifying your budget because every month is going to be different. Most of your major bills will be consistent month to month, so that'll be easy. For instance, since Winston and I have been doing a budget for a while, we know our food and other categories will generally stay the same month to month. But what's important is looking at the month ahead and anticipating what you have coming up *that would be different* from the month before, like buying Christmas presents, doing some home repairs, a scheduled doctor's visit, or paying for a trip.

Write It Down

Second, write your budget down. Don't rely on your memory or your ability to do the math in your head. You can do this on a simple sheet of paper, on your computer, on your phone, or even through a website or online budgeting tool (like the only one I recommend, EveryDollar.com). No matter where you choose to physically put your budget, it needs to be somewhere you can easily access it and review it throughout the month.

Put Every Dollar in a Category

My favorite type of budget is a zero-based budget. It truly is the most effective way to plan your spending. This type of budget means you'll need to anticipate your income and assign every single dollar to a category. Don't worry, this really isn't that complicated. It can be as simple as writing your monthly income at the top of a sheet of paper, with every monthly expense written under it. All your giving and saving, all your debt payments (hopefully none!), all your utilities, and all the pesky little things that sneak up on us throughout the month. Do your best to plan ahead, and spend that income right down the page until you get to zero. When you hit zero, guess what? You're done. You can't keep spending because you don't have any money left. And debt isn't an option anymore, right?

Zero-based budgeting eliminates the ambiguity that comes with money—so you can have the confidence you need to know you're *taking control of your money* instead of letting your money *take control of you*. If you leave any money sitting in your account without assigning it to a category, it will disappear. Every dollar has to be accounted for. A zero-based budget will tell your money what to do.

KEEP IT SIMPLE: GIVE, SAVE, SPEND

A budget doesn't have to be a complex set of spreadsheets with embedded formulas and pivot tables. All you need to do is organize your budget into three simple areas: *give*, *save*, and *spend*.

These three categories are virtually bulletproof.

Give

Giving should be at the top of your budget. It's the first thing you do with your money. That throws a lot of people off at first, and I get it. If we're talking about how to make your money go further, it can seem strange to start by giving your money away!

But there are some key principles at work here.

People who are givers tend to thrive. When you give to others, you become less focused on yourself and more focused on the people and needs around you. You become generous, and generous people tend to have a better quality of life than those who believe life is all about the endless pursuit of *more*. These people seem to do better in their jobs, finances, marriages, and just about every area of their lives.

Giving is a key character trait of people who win with money. It's so important, in fact, that I've made it one of the seven money habits we're covering in this book. We'll talk about it a lot more later.

Save

Your second category should be saving. There may be a few different line items related to savings for you in your budget. Maybe you're saving for a starter emergency fund of $1,000. Maybe you're saving for a vacation you're going to take in six months. Maybe you need to replace a car in a year or two. Brainstorm all the areas where you need to save, and decide how much you'll contribute each month. From retirement to Christmas, saving money will help you navigate life without feeling out of control.

You might be in a place financially where you have no wiggle room at all. The idea of giving or saving may feel completely out of reach right now. Continue writing out the budget and find places where you can cut so you have the ability to give and save. The dollar amount isn't important at this point; it's more about where you're placing your priorities. You may not have a lot of money to give or save today, but making these the first two items on your budget will ensure that you do it as soon as you are able. Remember, we're talking about developing healthy money habits to last a lifetime. If you want to develop a good saving habit, you need to practice!

Spend

The final category is spending.

This is where you're going to list out all of your expenses in life. Of course, there are going to be priorities. Make sure you have four basic areas covered before you do anything else:

1. *Food.* This is your grocery money. Some people include money for restaurants here, too, and that's fine if you want to. The key here, though—especially if money's tight or if you're getting out of debt—is that you need good meals to keep you strong and healthy. Of course, that doesn't mean steak and lobster every night, so be reasonable here!

2. *Housing/Utilities.* This can be your rent or mortgage payment, your heating bill, electricity, water, and so on. We're just talking about the necessities here, however. This *does not* include 900 cable channels! We'll get to that later.

3. *Clothes.* This includes money for your clothes and clothes for your children. Again, this should just cover the basics to start, but it's reasonable to expect your children to grow. If you want to add some more expensive pieces to your wardrobe, plan for the basics first, then finish out the rest of your normal monthly expenses. If there's money left, then come back and beef up your clothes category.

4. *Transportation.* This will include your gas, insurance, and maintenance, or, if you don't have a car, money for transit.

We call these the Four Walls. Those are your top priorities because you need to have food to eat, a roof over your head, clothes to wear, and transportation to take you where you need to go.

Food, shelter, clothes, and transportation can be covered by the bare essentials. If there is extra money in your budget and you want to bump up your spending in any of these categories, consider the wisdom in doing that. Down the road, you'll be able to say yes to these upgrades more often. But if you're buried under car payments, credit card bills, and student loans, now is not the time for luxuries. It's time to stick to the essentials.

Once you have those four basic areas covered, move down to other areas where you spend money—like insurance, cable, entertainment, and, of course, room for miscellaneous expenses. Life is going to happen. You're going to be asked to help throw a friend's wedding shower, or your family will be invited to a birthday party at the last minute, or your kids will take team pictures every soccer season. Things are going to come up that you didn't expect, or simply forgot about, so the miscellaneous category is there to catch the slack on those things.

If you have debt payments, don't forget those. List those out as well. We covered how to organize your debt snowball earlier in the book, so go back and review that if you're not sure how to budget your debts.

This is the part of your budget where you choose how to spend your money. Yes, you *choose*. For you to live the kind of life you want to live, you have to make choices. Maybe you budget more for groceries because you choose to shop at an organic grocery store. That means you will have to budget less in another category. Or if you are saving for a new set of golf clubs or a new purse, you'll have to budget to cover those purchases, which means you'll have less money for other things you might want to do. The key here is your ability to choose. Your money can only do what you tell it to do, so you have to be intentional and wise with those choices. That not only gives you control of your money but also your life.

For all the stress and dread that's often associated with budgeting, the truth is that it's just not that complicated. What goes in the budget is totally up to you. You're the boss—until it's on the paper. Once you write it down and everyone who has a stake in the plan agrees, then the budget is in charge. Yes, you can tweak it here and there as needed, but if you're married, your spouse has to be involved in the change. And, of course, since this is a *zero*-based budget, if you increase one spending category, you've got to cut that amount out of another. You can't run your budget negative!

CASH IS AMAZING

One of the best tools you can use to keep your budget on track is cash. That's right: cold, hard cash. Did you know stores still accept this? I'm kidding, but my point is: if you tend to overspend in some specific areas when using your debit card, nothing will bring your spending back in line faster than using actual cash.

Clips and Envelopes

The envelope system has been around for decades; maybe you've heard of it. I've given it my own spin and call it the clip system. I use small binder clips (the kind you find at an office supply store) to keep my cash in my wallet separated by category. I like this because I can still use my wallet instead of carrying around actual envelopes.

The clip system works like this. Let's say you have budgeted $400 for groceries every month. When you get paid, you dedicate a clip for groceries and take $400 cash out of the bank. Then, when you go to the grocery store, you use that cash to pay for the groceries. Having cash for a few budget items is great, because you always know exactly how much you have left to spend in each category each month.

The categories I personally use with my clip system are groceries, restaurants, personal spending money (nails, hair, etc.), clothes, and miscellaneous. Winston cashes out his personal spending money and what he wants to spend at Home Depot. That's right: we have a Home Depot line on our monthly budget.

Don't miss that, by the way. Winston and I each budget a set amount of cash for our personal, miscellaneous expenses. I don't care what you call it—fun money, pocket cash, personal money, whatever. The main thing is that we plan for those miscellaneous things we know we're going to want to do or buy in a given month. Then, when we each get that cash out of the bank, we don't worry about what the other person is doing with it. You need to be unified with your money as a couple, but you don't have to lose your individual identity or talk about every dollar you spend on yourself.

Spending Less

There's an added benefit to using cash for some categories: *you end up spending less.* When Winston and I go out for a nice dinner and I get our restaurant cash out, it makes me think twice about ordering an appetizer. It's hard to physically hand over a $10 bill for an extra large bowl of guacamole. And you already know how much I love guacamole.

I find this to be true even when I'm shopping. When I hand over $50 in cash for a blouse, there is an exchange that happens. I have to let go of that $50 bill in order to take the item home. The exchange is real, so you feel it. If you get used to carrying cash around, you kind of want to hang on to it. You just don't get that emotional connection to your money if you swipe a card for every purchase. My debit card is *always* in my wallet. If I buy something with the debit card, I take the item *and* the card home. But when I use cash, I have to leave something behind. Don't underestimate the emotional punch you get from that.

Your Own Pre-Approval

Another reason I love the clip system is that it gives me tangible permission to spend. When I have money in my restaurant clip, I can go out to lunch with a friend and not feel guilty about spending that money. Or if I have money in my clothing category, I can go shopping and not question if this money should be used for something else. It's guilt-free spending because it's allocated specifically for shopping.

I encourage you to give this a try. The clip system keeps you accountable. Not only does it allow you to visually see what you can spend, but it also shows you when you have to stop spending.

COMMON BUDGET CHALLENGES

Like anything new you start doing, budgeting won't feel normal at first. The most important thing is to keep at it. And know that it will get easier with practice. Changing your habits takes time; it doesn't happen immediately. And there are a couple of challenges I've seen people face as they first start their new budgeting lifestyles. Let's take a minute to look at those so you'll be ready for them if they pop up for you.

Giving Up Too Soon

A major problem I see when people start doing a budget for the first time is they give up too early. The first month usually ends up being a disaster. They blow the budget in the first week and think, *Okay. This is never going to work, so I should just give up.* Please don't! It will take time, but it will work.

Give yourself three months for your budget to start working smoothly. The first month will be rough. Expect that. Just go ahead and own it. When Winston and I first started budgeting together, it was hard—and that was after doing a lot of this stuff my whole life! I remember it not working the first month and getting frustrated, but we kept at it and it started to come together. This can be true for you too. *Just keep doing it.*

Not only are you trying something new for the first time, but you also may have no idea how much money you spend on certain things. Look at your bank account statements and add up each expense category. Get an average of what you spent in each area over the last couple of months. Granted, this may make you want to puke because you will come face to face with your actual spending—maybe for the first time. Looking this closely can be scary, but it's necessary.

Living on More Than You Make

The good news here is that your situation may not be as bad as you think. Quite often people will say, "I was terrified to look at all the bills and write down how much money we actually spend every month, but, once I did it, I realized it wasn't as out of reach as I had thought."

Thomas Jefferson said, "Never spend your money before you have it." That simply means, live on what you make. A budget isn't going to bring you new money; it will just help you manage the money you have. For some people, when they sit down and write out where their money goes, they see that they actually make plenty of money to do everything they want. They realize they've just been sloppy. But others may see there isn't enough money coming in. If that is the case for you, you have an income problem, not a budget problem. The first thing to do is to *cut, cut, cut.* Don't spend any more money than you have available to spend. If you still come up short, then you have to look at some other options.

You can't live life spending more than you make. If you've made all the cuts you can and still don't have enough to get any traction, there's really only one other option: you need to make more money. That may mean finding another job, making a career change, working overtime, or taking on an extra job. If you are married and one of you stays at home, maybe that person can go back to work or create a way to generate some income from home.

Find some way to make that extra income. This may not be a solution you like or enjoy. You may end up doing something you don't necessarily want to do. It might mean being away from the kids for longer than you'd like or working a job you might not be passionate about. Keep in mind, though, this isn't forever. This situation is temporary—especially if most of your money is going out the door in debt payments that you're paying off.

Of course, another trouble spot is failing to communicate and agree with your spouse about the budget. This one is huge! In fact, we're going to spend a whole chapter talking about how to make sure you keep the "happily" in "happily married" when it comes to your money.

ELECTRONIC TRACKING

I'm a fan of cash, and I love my clip system. But I'm also a fan of debit cards. Not credit cards. *Debit* cards. A debit card is 100 percent okay to use because you're using your money. It's coming directly out of your checking account. You aren't borrowing money from the bank like you are with a credit card.

Debit Cards
A debit card is absolutely the way to go if you want the convenience of plastic. It doesn't really have the initial sting that comes with

using cash, but at least you still know that actual money is being pulled from your bank account every time you use the card.

Most people prefer using a debit card over cash because it's easier to handle and you don't have to worry about carrying around a wad of bills. If you're just starting out this budgeting process, try the clip system for some categories instead of swiping your debit card. If you are a natural spender, cash can be a good friend and accountability partner.

Online Banking

The days of using a paper check register are essentially gone for most people. Online banking is alive and well. So use it! This gives you great visibility into what's going on with your money. Just be sure to reconcile your checking account against receipts after you use your debit card. Winston checks our checking account pretty much every day. He's one of those high-detail people, remember? But we both know what our budget is and what we have to spend.

If you don't stay on top of your checking account balance, you can still spend beyond the money in your account. That's called an overdraft. It's possible and much easier to do than you might think. The bank doesn't have much of an incentive to prevent you from overdrafting your account. In fact, they make a ton of money on the fees when you overdraft, and they are more than happy to charge you. So be on guard.

Also keep in mind that one mistake could trigger a series of overdrafts depending on how different checks and charges hit your account, and you'll owe a big fee for every single overdraft. This one is a killer, so beware. Find an easy way to keep tabs on your checking account balance. Just a little detailed focus and some knowledge of what you have in the account will keep you from going into the red.

Also, it's a smart move to keep a little buffer cash in your checking account. An extra $100 will cover the accidental oversight or additional fee you weren't expecting. A zero-based budget absolutely does not mean that you need to run your bank account down to zero, so keep a little padding in there to stay safe.

SPEND WITH CONFIDENCE

Telling your money what to do doesn't have to be complicated or boring. Living within your means is all about being clear and intentional about how you'll use your money. This will help you spend with confidence, knowing you've funded every important category. There won't be this nagging voice in the back of your head questioning every purchase and wondering if you actually have the money to spend. What a relief! Plus, your budget can be as simple as a sheet of paper or, if you'd rather do it online or on your phone, there are some great budgeting tools available like EveryDollar.com.

Your budget is the path to freedom and fun. Seriously! Never forget that a budget gives you permission to spend. This is a critical, essential habit you need to build for living the life you want.

Talk About Money (Even When It's Hard)

8

Marry Your Money

L et's take a walk down memory lane. Do you remember when
social media was first starting out? The first main network in
my life was Facebook, back when Facebook was just for college students. I remember receiving my college email address and being so
excited that I could set up a Facebook account. As soon as I logged
in the first time, I was hooked. I started scanning through the different friend suggestions. One particular guy's profile caught my
eye immediately: Winston Cruze. I said to myself, *Wow. I'd like to
meet him.*

Winston's sister, Charlotte, and I became friends that year—and,
no, not because I thought her older brother was good-looking! Over
the next couple years, I saw Winston from time to time, and those
meetings were always laid back and comfortable. He eventually asked
me out, and over time we fell in love. We started to talk about getting
married and everything that entailed, including money.

COMPATIBILITY MATTERS

One of the things I love about healthy dating relationships is that so much gets revealed when the couple starts talking about important things like faith, family, and money. The more time they spend together, the more likely they are to discover each other's strengths, passions, and values.

Winston and I had been dating for a little more than two years when my dad invited us to participate together in a conference he designed for small-business owners called EntreLeadership.

Part of preparing for this conference included taking a formal personality profile assessment called DiSC. There are many personality tests out there, but DiSC is one of my favorites. DiSC identifies four quadrants of personality styles: D–Dominant, I–Influential, S–Steady, C–Compliant.

D personalities are hard-driving and task-oriented. I personalities are the life of the party, love people, and love being social. S personalities are loyal, calm, rational, and sensitive to people around them. C personalities are process- and detail-oriented.

When you complete the assessment, you get a detailed document that shows you where you fall in each of the four areas. Winston is a high C while I am a high I. Being around people energizes me, but social events can be draining for him. He loves details and processes, but I have no interest in knowing all the details about every little thing. We're both pretty good at making decisions, but we go about it in very different ways. We balance each other out pretty well.

Because we went through this assessment process in our dating relationship, the experience gave us a lot of significant insights into how we were going to interact with each other—and what speed bumps we might encounter along the way. Assessments like these shouldn't replace premarital counseling, but they did give us a framework to better understand how and why we are different.

That meant we could better learn how to work together, even if we were coming at a situation from different perspectives.

Opposites Attract

As I travel and meet people all around the country, I see how important it is to understand and acknowledge our own biases, assumptions, and expectations. This is especially true when it comes to money. If you've been married for more than two minutes, you know that one spouse is probably more of a spender than a saver (and vice-versa). One may love to do budgets, while the other likes making money decisions on the fly. One may have a long-term focus, while the other wants to just live in the moment.

That's normal.

I'm the natural spender in my marriage, and Winston is the natural saver. Now I say *natural*, but everyone has the ability to do both. For most people, they just naturally gravitate to one or the other. One preference is simply more dominant than the other. If all you do is spend money, then you have no control, no boundaries, and will end up broke. Bad news for us spenders! But if all you do is save money, then you will miss out on a lot of fun you could be having. That's no good either. While you absolutely need to make saving a habit and a key part of your financial plan, you also need to enjoy all your hard work. There's room in your life for both.

Being a natural spender or natural saver is not right or wrong. There's no "right" way to be. These are simply different bents when it comes to people and how they handle their money—part of what makes you who you are. As you grow in your understanding of money and create a plan for yourself, you will eventually find a balance between the two.

There are two more types we can add to the mix: the planner and the partier. The planner loves doing the budget. This person tends to be more organized, loves details, likes feeling in control, and tends to get stressed out if he or she doesn't have a plan for everything. The partier tends to be more big-picture minded and may see budgets as restricting or confining. Generally speaking, as long as partiers have the money to take care of the basics and have a little fun, they're happy.

Mix and Match

Teaching about personal finance is what I do for a living, which includes speaking, writing, and coaching others to develop better money habits. Most people might assume, then, that I'm the planner and Winston is the partier in our relationship. But it's just the opposite.

While Winston loves doing the budget, it's still something I have to push myself to do. I know it's crucial for winning with money, but that doesn't necessarily mean that I am doing backflips to work on a budget every month. Thankfully, though, Winston truly enjoys it.

It's important to note that savers are not always planners, and spenders are not always partiers. You can be a saver and feel no need for a budget. You can be a spender and plan everything. We are actually great friends with a couple in which the husband is the spender and the planner and the wife is the saver and the partier. Obviously, these personality types can come together and succeed in handling money.

POTENTIAL PROBLEM AREAS

If you're married, money can cause a great deal of stress in your relationship. In fact, a recent study found that "arguments about money are by far the top predictor of divorce. It's not children, sex, in-laws or anything else. It's money—for both men and women."[1] There is a boatload of potential problems when it comes to marriage and money. You may be facing some of these right now. A few of these challenges may be simple to fix, while other problems might take more time and even some outside help.

Money fights and money problems are painful. If you and your spouse are struggling to work together as a team, you know how difficult it can be to not agree on money. Perhaps the single most important thing you can do for the sake of your marriage is to work together so that you can be on the same page about your money.

If you're not married but hope to marry someday, start practicing these principles now with someone you trust. Even if you never marry, this information will challenge you to take a good, hard look at all the emotions you have around money and understand how those emotions affect the decisions that you make.

Separate or Joint Accounts?

Want to know one of the biggest reasons married couples fail to win with money? Separate accounts. If each spouse earns an income, he may have his paycheck going into *his* account, and she may have her paycheck going into *her* account. Then, if they do any planning at all, they try to divvy up responsibility. I hear this all the time: "Oh, he pays the power bill, and I pay the cable bill." I can't stress enough how huge a mistake this is. Keeping your accounts separate is one of the most effective ways to wreck your financial life—and maybe even your marriage. Why would you even take that risk?

When you stand in front of God, your family, friends, and the love of your life and someone says, "I now pronounce you husband and wife," you're married. That declaration means you are inseparable; you are one. You go from living your own life to being unified with another person. You're now in a lifelong, committed relationship, and it's no longer only about you. You're not two business partners coming into a deal. You're one unit.

If you believe that in all other areas of life, why would you draw the line at money? You have to be *one* in every area of life to have a successful and healthy marriage. While remaining a unique individual, your value systems and goals must line up with one another. Otherwise, you'll end up living two separate lives, and that's when your relationship becomes simply a tax status—not a marriage.

In their book *The Complete Marriage Book*, Drs. David and Jan Stoop say, "Prior to marriage, many of us had to answer only to ourselves. A major shift occurred as we began our married life. We are now accountable to each other. How do you react when someone limits you? This is where 'iron sharpens iron' (Proverbs 27:17) and the sparks begin to fly."[2] Money is an outward expression of an inward commitment. You either love someone with everything you are or you don't. You can't have the commitment and trust required to be married for the long haul if you draw the line at money.

How you use your money *always* reveals your priorities. That's because money is never just about money. Money reveals what you truly value in life. Your money not only represents your value system, but it also reveals your goals, fears, and dreams. Being on the same page and unified together in all areas of life is essential—and that absolutely includes your checking account.

What's Yours and What's Mine

The popular "that's yours and this is mine" mind-set is destructive in relationships. If you're married, there should be no such thing as *my* money or *your* money; it's *our* money. It doesn't matter who brings in the paycheck or who makes more than the other. When the paycheck hits the bank account, you have to look at it as *our* money. When you make that shift, you'll start to feel even more unified with your spouse.

If you've never had a joint checking account before, it can seem scary. Everything you do with money becomes visible. Suddenly you're accountable to someone else about what you spend. Someone else is taking a peek inside an area of your life that was once totally private. If you've never been there before, that's a pretty vulnerable place to be—but that vulnerability builds trust, which only improves your relationship over time.

One benefit of having a single checking account is that it forces you to communicate with one another. It might be a little painful at first because you may not have had these conversations before. These discussions open the door to see what you and your spouse are doing with money and will encourage you to be accountable to someone else before you make a significant purchase.

One Warning

It's worth mentioning here that, yes, I'm aware there are some extreme situations when a joint account may not make sense. Some spouses may have legitimate concerns about trusting their partner on financial matters because of past or present behavior. If your spouse is a gambling addict, for example, he or she probably shouldn't have full access to the family finances.

Don't stop using your brain. Common sense prevails. If there is something immoral or irresponsible going on (like drug addiction, marital infidelity, etc.), then you need to deal with those realities before joining accounts. That's not really a money problem; that's more of a marriage problem. Get help, rebuild the trust, and then get your money back together as soon as you can.

LIVE AND LEARN

Once you join your accounts, it will become more obvious than ever who is the partier and who is the planner. Winston checks our account all the time. He loves digging into the details and wants to make sure everything is accurate. While I check our account regularly, I don't feel the pressure to look at it every day. I know the budget, I have my cash clip system for some expenses, and I know where my money is going. I simply trust the system.

A quick note to the planners here: Make sure the partier has all the necessary log-in information for your checking account. They may not check in as much as you do, but this will increase their sense of ownership in the process. A quick note to the partiers: for the sake of communication and for your own knowledge, check in on what's happening in the accounts at least once a month, enough to feel comfortable with the system and to know what is going on.

Secret Shopping for Gifts

One excuse I often hear for keeping separate accounts is to keep gift giving a secret. "I don't want to combine our accounts because then I can't buy my wife a gift. She'll see how much I spent and where I spent it, and it will ruin the surprise." Let's be real here. This is something that may happen two or three times a year. Don't put off combining your accounts and missing out on all of the benefits for something that only happens at Christmas, on your anniversary, and on birthdays.

If you want to buy your spouse a gift, just tell him or her what's going on. When my birthday is coming up, Winston will say, "Hey, I'm going to cash out some money because your birthday is coming up." I know he is going to buy me a gift, so it's no surprise that he needs some money for that purchase. On Winston's last birthday he wanted a sound bar for our TV in our living room. I printed out a picture of one and taped it to the inside of his birthday card. That way he could pick out the exact one he wanted. If you're shopping online, another option is to use cash to buy a gift card so that your spouse won't see the individual transaction come through the checking account. If you're going to buy something from Amazon, for example, use cash to buy an Amazon gift card at the store. You can even buy a Visa or MasterCard gift card with cash and use that for online shopping—just be sure to avoid the ones that try to charge you an activation fee before you can use the gift card.

I know this creates a bit of an inconvenience a couple of times a year, but in the grand scope of your marriage, it's just not that big of a deal. Remember earlier when we talked about the tradeoffs sometimes required when creating healthy money habits? Well, this is one of those times. Endure the extra hassle when it comes to surprises and gifts for your spouse. Take advantage of the major benefits of having one account and get creative when you need to.

Accounts You Shouldn't Combine

Both your names should appear on the family checking, savings, and money market accounts. These are the easy ones to combine. However, if you run a business on the side, you want to keep your business bank account separate from your personal account. It's fine if both spouses are on the business account; just don't mix your personal and your business money. That creates a huge mess at tax time.

Second, don't combine your retirement accounts—most banks won't allow you to do this anyway. Roth IRA, 401(k), or 403(b) accounts are all associated with an individual, with the option of listing a spouse as a beneficiary. Separating retirement accounts will allow you to take full advantage of maxing those out individually. But, again, each person needs total visibility on all the retirement accounts. I can't stress enough how important it is to have open, honest, and clear lines of communication around what is going on with every aspect of your financial situation.

Of course, do not combine your accounts until you're married. There have been so many horror stories of couples who intended to get married and combined accounts to help pay off the other's bills and debts—only to break up in the end. Until you are married, keep your accounts separate. The day you say "I do," though, combine your accounts *and* your debts. In relationships where one person is in debt during the engagement, the other can save up money to put toward that debt snowball, but they should not write that check for their future spouse's debt until after they say "I do."

Managing the Spending Wars

Don't fall into a "competitive spending" mind-set—meaning, if one person makes a purchase, that justifies a comparable purchase by the other. This idea of equal spending is a dangerous one. This can quickly become a slippery slope of outspending one another. If each person spends an equal amount as the other, that means you double the cost of every personal purchase. Even worse, you cultivate the idea of keeping score in your marriage, which will eat away at your relationship over time.

Competitive spending is grounded in a skewed view of fairness. I have learned that fair is not always equal, and equal is not always fair. This is true in just about every area of life. Each partner has different financial needs at different times. One month he will need to replace his laptop. Another month, she'll need a new cell phone. You can't get to the end of the year and try to find perfect equality in each person's spending. That's just not how life—or money—works.

Some people also buy into the idea that whoever *earns* the money has exclusive rights to decide what they get to do with it. This usually sounds like, "It's *my* money! You can't tell me how to spend it, and you shouldn't expect me to give you any of it!" Absolutely not. If you earn a big commission check one month, is it okay for you to enjoy some of it? Yes, of course. It's also okay for your spouse to enjoy some of it. And it's even okay for your spouse to enjoy *all* of it if that's what's appropriate at that time.

You can't forget family financial goals during those times either. If a couple is thousands of dollars in debt with no savings and he wants to go spend his big commission check on new clothes or golf clubs, that just wouldn't be wise. The family has bigger priorities than his golf game. Sorry to all you golfers out there! The wife in that situation shouldn't feel bad about pushing back against that purchase. In fact, I think she has an obligation to throw a flag here, even if she *wants* her husband to be able to enjoy some new clubs. You can't justify or enable irresponsible spending habits because you feel like someone deserves it.

Teamwork Through Budgeting

You can prevent any of the situations above by doing a budget together. When you make a plan for every dollar together, you're setting priorities and giving yourselves permission to spend in specific ways that lead to your goal. The budget you do together will keep your lives and dreams in a healthy balance with one another. Doing a budget together also kills the mind-set that says, "I make more, so I can spend more." This is an unhealthy—not to mention destructive—way of looking at your money. Say good-bye to the "I deserve it" attitude at the wedding ceremony.

A great way to think about this is to view all income as *budgeted* income. Nothing is off the table. Bonuses, tax refunds, and side-project money from both spouses all flow into one big pile of cash that sits at the top of your budget ready to be spent on paper *first*. That way it's all going to be accounted for in the budget you will do together.

The bottom line is this: someone is always going to make more in any marriage. Avoid focusing on your income and your spouse's income as separate entities. The challenge is to get rid of the "this is *my* income" mentality and have a unified mind-set. The money that comes into your home has to be seen as one combined income. Looking at money this way will cause an emotional shift in your thinking that will impact your money habits—and your marriage— in a positive and powerful way.

MARRIAGE IS BUILT ON COMMUNICATION

Language shapes how we view other people and the world around us. That's why I've pushed hard on your thinking, attitude, and the conversations you're having with your spouse. If you're budgeting together, then you're talking about money together. I can tell you from personal experience that it's worth pressing through those conversations even though it takes a lot of energy and it isn't always easy.

Winston and I still hit the occasional speed bump when it comes to dealing with our money.

We struggle with the same things every married couple struggles with. Once in a while, we need to hit reset on some things. That makes up the essence of a healthy marriage—a lifetime of learning how to work together, especially as circumstances change.

We've found that our marriage is stronger and our life together is sweeter because we believe and behave in ways that *make us one*. We were taught this long before we were married. We were both lucky to have had parents who modeled this for us growing up. In our families of origin, no matter who brought in the paycheck, there was always an "our money" approach to financial matters.

When Winston and I talk about our income, I don't even think about what *I* make versus what *he* makes. I only care about what *we* make. We're a team, and the team is going to win together. We didn't start talking about money by accident. You won't either. You have to be intentional and deliberate when it comes to talking about money—even when it's hard.

9

Important Conversations

I've mentioned how much I love New York City. I go there as often as I can, usually for work. Everything about that city is great: the food, the shows, and, of course, the shopping. I feel like every time I'm there, the Holy Spirit whispers to me, *You should be living here.* Ironically, my husband says he hears the same thing when he is in a duck blind, so Nashville it is!

Now, you need to understand something. Winston and I have had a line item in our budget for clothes from day one. It's something I love to spend money on, so we plan for it.

I happened to be shopping one afternoon on a recent trip to NYC. I couldn't believe how many great sales there were! You probably know where this is going. Yep—I busted the budget. Now, normally, I would text Winston to let him know I was buying some clothes. This helps me stay accountable. This particular time, though, for whatever reason, I didn't. I ended up spending about $250 more than I meant to.

As the day passed, the reality of how much I spent set in. I couldn't stand it anymore. I texted Winston about my spending. He assured me it was no big deal. We had the extra money. But it was a big deal for me because I felt like I was carrying a big secret around with me, and I didn't like how that felt. That's when it hit me how much I rely on quality communication about money with my husband. When it was missing, even just for one shopping trip on a New York City afternoon, I felt disconnected from my marriage. That may sound dramatic, but it's true. I hate feeling like Winston and I are on different pages. And that's why we talk about money.

You have to talk about money with your spouse if you want to get on the same page. If you don't, you are setting yourself up for some relationship-straining situations.

FINANCIAL INFIDELITY

When I realized my oversight that day, I told Winston right away. I had to! I was driving myself crazy! Some couples, though, hold on to those secrets for far too long. One of the most painful problems I see with married couples is financial infidelity. This happens when one spouse hides purchases, accounts, or money from their partner. This can present itself in ways like a secret credit card, a hidden bank account "just in case" the marriage goes south, or chronic issues like gambling.

This type of behavior can devastate a marriage. The pain and feelings of betrayal are so severe that some people think it's comparable to sexual infidelity—because of all the lying, mistrust, sneaking around, and dishonesty that's needed for this kind of thing to happen. Anytime you purposefully hide something money-related from your spouse, that's financial infidelity.

Infidelity vs. Irresponsibility

Let's not get too crazy here, however. There is a difference between *infidelity* and *irresponsibility*. A woman once told me, "My husband was financially unfaithful to me! He went out to lunch six times last month and didn't tell me about it!" In that case I'd give him the benefit of the doubt. He probably simply forgot to mention these lunches to his wife. I wouldn't consider that to be infidelity. Sloppy? Sure. Forgetful? No doubt. But infidelity? Not really.

If, on the other hand, he spent hundreds of dollars taking big groups of people out and purposefully hid that information from her, then, yes, that might be financial infidelity. But grabbing a burger with coworkers and not mentioning it would not qualify.

How do you know if you're skirting the line between irresponsibility and infidelity? I think it's a matter of intention. If there's ever a point when you feel the need to hide a purchase because of how you think your spouse will react, or if you simply don't want your spouse to know about something you bought, then you're in the danger zone. Something's going on with you or in your marriage that you need to dig into.

Have you spent money you agreed you wouldn't spend? Then you have to own up to that mistake and tell your spouse right away. If talking about money isn't already a habit in your marriage, it's time to sit down together and get the communication started. The more you avoid the money discussion, the more likely it is to begin to splinter your trust and confidence in each other.

Preventing Relationship Damage

True financial infidelity will cause significant damage to your marriage. If you're there right now, choose to take the difficult but necessary steps to bring it out into the open. Get some competent help. Bring in a third party like a marriage counselor, pastor, or someone else you both trust.

Like I said before, if taken to extremes, financial infidelity can feel like an affair, so you need to treat it seriously. At that point it becomes more of a *marriage* problem than a *money* problem. And you can't budget your way out of a broken marriage. If you're the one committing financial infidelity, ask yourself: *Why do I feel the need to hide this? What is the motivation behind wanting to sneak around?* Face that unhealthy attitude and come clean. This will slowly lead to better communication on priorities you both agree upon.

In previous chapters, we've talked a lot about budgeting together and having joint bank accounts. We've talked about why each partner needs full visibility and access into everything, and we've covered why it's important for spouses to approach their finances as a team. If you're doing all that and taking it seriously, financial infidelity is much less likely to happen. From a relational standpoint, I've found that couples who work together on their money are generally closer, so the trust factor is much higher. And from a practical standpoint, it's just hard to hide purchases from a spouse who is regularly checking the budget and looking at the bank account online. You've built in safeguards that help protect against one spouse going rogue with the money.

Now, you may be reading this and know for certain that something is going on with your spouse. Maybe you've become convinced of some serious financial infidelity, and you aren't sure what to do. This may feel like you're trying to hold back a tidal wave of uncertainty and anxiety. If you're dealing with a well-established pattern of behavior, be smart about it. Do what you need to do to protect your health and finances. In the face of extraordinary financial misbehavior, you may have to temporarily go back to separate checking accounts. We talked about some reasons for doing so in the last chapter. This is a time when it would be necessary to protect yourself, so don't feel bad about doing it. This doesn't close the door forever, though. With effort and focus, you and your spouse can get back on track, work through it, and get past it for good.

LEAVE NOTHING OFF THE TABLE

Love puts no limits on topics for conversation—that includes money. While financial infidelity can be devastating, you don't have to let it get that far. The key to getting on the same page is to budget together. It may seem like a simple answer, but it is the answer to most money problems in marriage.

Find a time and place to do this. Make sure you both are present. This can be at a restaurant, your kitchen table, or on the back porch. Winston and I usually do our monthly budget while we relax on the couch together. Find a place and a time before the next month begins to sit down and make it your budget night.

Remove any distractions. Turn off the TV. Make sure the kids won't interrupt you. If necessary, go out on a budget date and make talking about money a little more fun. Whatever you have to do to make this time appealing to you both, do it.

Listen, Don't Tell

When two people bring their own histories, views, and experiences into a marriage, it's easy to understand why so many couples argue about money all the time. In his book *The Meaning of Money in Marriage*, David Augsburger said, "The handling of finances is one of the major emotional battlegrounds of any marriage. Lack of finances is seldom the issue. The root problem seems to be an unrealistic and immature view of money." The only real cure for this potential land mine is open and honest communication.

Keep in mind that you both have an opinion when it comes to money matters in the relationship. You are not the only one with a perspective on the issues. That can be easy to forget. That's why it's important to listen first and speak later.

Actively listen to what your spouse has to say. Paraphrase his or her concerns in your own words. Because money usually carries an emotional response with it, you'll discover what's important and what creates stress for your spouse. If you ever feel a sense of hesitation or fear going into a budget conversation, get that out on the table too. Oftentimes, this mild dread is perfectly normal when you do new things. Don't let that stop you. Push through it.

While we should never let feelings stop us from talking about money, we should be aware of how those filters influence our reactions to money conversations. She might be nervous or scared. He might have his pride knocked down. Her security could be rattled. His self-esteem could be low. Be aware of how sensitive this process can be to your spouse.

Remember, every relationship has a planner and a partier. Both have a role to play in how you decide to use money. The planner is likely going to love this discussion because it will be a time to dig down into the details. The partier is likely to show a bit more resistance.

If you are the planner, here's a word of caution: Don't approach the partier, hand him or her the budget, and say, "Here is the budget. You don't need to look over it; it's done and it's correct." Be prepared to listen to the partier and their thoughts about how money in the budget should be spent. While you may be the more organized of the two of you, you still need to get the partier's input.

Now if you are the partier like I am, you have to bring two things to the budget meeting: your opinion and maturity. Leave statements like, "I want to spend half of our money on clothes" at the door. Or worse, don't just say, "Sure, that looks fine. Whatever you want to do." Speak up and offer your opinion to the conversation.

The budget needs to be visual so you both can see it. Write it down or use a budgeting app like EveryDollar.com. This needs to be done before the month begins. And you need a new budget every month, even if most of the numbers are similar month to month.

There are many benefits when you create a budget together. When you're agreeing on where your money is going, it will unify the two of you in ways you may not have experienced before. There will be a sense of harmony where there used to be tension. You get to agree on where you are going in life together—and on where your dreams will take you. Over time you may find that *talking* about the money is more valuable than the money itself.

Dream Together

Winston and I often have dinners together when we just talk about what we want life to be like in the future. We've done this from the beginning of our marriage. Shortly before one of these conversations early in our marriage, Winston was just getting into real estate. He started dreaming about the day when we could buy a small property with cash and rent it out. We talked about going to Disney once we had kids. We even imagined what we'd like retirement to look like for the both of us. As we talked, the conversation kept building on itself.

After about an hour of talking about all the things we wanted to do and all the places we wanted to go, we suddenly snapped back to reality. We wondered if we were being a little shallow talking about all of this for so long, but then it struck us: no, we weren't being superficial—we were dreaming, and we were doing it *together*. That conversation was huge for us as we were starting our life together.

Have talks like this with your spouse! Just dream. Go out on a date and have fun thinking about your future together. It's amazing how much joy there is in working together toward the same goal in life. These types of conversations can bring focus, purpose, and meaning to life. They make you feel like you're taking control of your life rather than letting life control you—that you're planning out *your life* together, and not just wishing you were living someone else's.

You can do this. Talk about money even when it's hard. Push through the uncomfortable conversations and get to the other side. My hope is that you and your spouse can get on the same page with your money and start to find a new level of unity in your marriage that you will not be able to experience any other way.

WHEN YOU'RE SINGLE

If you're single, there's a modified way to do this—same plan, different players. Find someone in your life who you can talk to about money. It's just as crucial for you to get caring, outside input on your budget as it is for someone who's married. This person should be someone you trust because you'll probably share some numbers you want to be kept confidential. And, obviously, you want to find someone who is good with money. This isn't really the place for a designer-loving, shopping-all-the-time girlfriend.

You should be comfortable sharing your budget with this person because they will help keep you accountable. Ask them to text you a few times a month to see how you've been doing with your money. It would be wise to choose someone who you could call before making a huge purchase, just to help you keep things in perspective. And make sure this person can celebrate the big wins in your life, like getting a raise or eliminating debt.

This person needs to love you enough to not be afraid to hurt your feelings. He or she needs to be able to say things like, "Cashing out your IRA to buy a boat is a stupid idea" or "New bedroom furniture is not an emergency!" You want someone who will speak money truth and wisdom into your purchases and decisions with money.

This person also needs to value what you value. If they think racking up credit card debt in order to raise your credit score is a good idea, then they may not understand your commitment to debt-free living. If you make it a priority to save for retirement but this person keeps telling you, "Go live your life; don't worry about the future!"—then find someone else.

When you're single, it's easy to do your own thing when it comes to your money. You don't have to ask about the things you want to buy. Sitting at home by yourself is not as fun as going out with friends, so plan for those nights out. It may be easy for you to overspend simply because your money decisions aren't impacting anyone else.

There's nothing inherently wrong with these things. Just make sure you budget for your lifestyle and that you're spending your money wisely. If you're out of debt and saving for the future, then make your eating-out category in your budget larger if you want. Just be intentional about the changes you make.

When You're Dating

When you're out on the first date, you probably shouldn't ask about the other person's income, car payments, or the amount of debt he or she has racked up. I'm no dating expert, but if you do, you probably won't get asked out on a second date, and you might come across as crazy. But if the relationship starts to get serious, it's important to start talking about money. Money is such a taboo subject for many people. The topic can be embarrassing, and it's definitely personal. Nevertheless, money-related issues need to be talked about extensively before marriage.

If bee stings were the number-one killer in your city, what would you do? You would read up on where bees live, what makes them sting, and what types of clothes you need to wear to protect yourself.

If this were true, everyone would be walking around in bee protective suits—and that would be considered "normal." You would talk about bees to your friends, family, and neighbors. There would be meetings about how to defend yourself against a bee sting. If the worst-case scenario happened and you actually got stung, there would be a plan in place to make sure you survived.

If you knew that money issues were one of the top killers of marriages, what would you do? You'd talk about it all the time—and then you'd make a plan!

When you're in a dating relationship that might lead to a long-term commitment, initiate the conversation. How the other person responds will help you make a wise decision about whether or not you'll move forward with the relationship. Eventually, you will want to share information with each other like how much you make, the amount of debt you would bring to the table, your goals for your money, and your top financial priorities. If you ultimately can't trust your boyfriend or girlfriend with these conversations, then I've got bad news: either you're not ready to get married or you haven't found the right person yet. That may be hard to hear, but it's the truth!

KIDS AND PARENTS

Many parents are hesitant to talk with their kids about money because they feel guilt or shame from their own past mistakes. If you're a parent, talk to your kids about money, even when it's hard. Teach them how money works. This is not the school's job, a counselor's job, or anyone else's job. It's your job.

One of my friends has an eight-year-old son who has more than $1,000 in his own savings account. It started as a challenge from my friend's husband to their son, who was five at the time. They opened up his own savings account and told him they would match every deposit until he reached a balance of $1,000. In just three years, their son met his goal and has more money in a savings account than many adults.

He is learning at an early age the power and excitement of watching his money grow over time. That doesn't happen by accident. This experience will shape his view and use of money for the rest of his life. So how exactly do you talk to your kids about money? It's pretty simple.

The Basics

Start with the basics. Teach them to work, give, save, and spend. Growing up, my parents never gave us an allowance. We were always on commission. You work, you get paid; you don't work, you don't get paid. This taught me from a young age that money comes from work—not from Mom and Dad's wallets.

Attach a specific amount of money to certain chores your kids do around the house, and let them earn their own money. Of course, every child needs to do some chores simply because they're part of a family, so I'm not suggesting paying them for *everything* they do around the house. But I encourage parents to attach a commission to some of those chores. With commissions, kids have to work for every dollar; that changes how they handle the money you pay them. When your children *earn* their money, they will give it differently, save it differently, and spend it differently because they feel more of an emotional connection to it.

Teach them to spend, save, and give *wisely*. Talk them through purchases. Explain the difference between quality verses quantity. Your influence on the next generation begins at home. Be the bridge your kids need to a better, brighter future where they can win with money even earlier in life than you did.

Teaching your children about money is most effective when you give them opportunities to work, give, save, and spend themselves. It gives them great practice before they enter the outside world. There also needs to be some conversations around money. As the parent, one of your jobs is to help shape your kids' expectations about the future. Help them visualize what it will look—and feel—like to save up and pay cash for a big purchase like their first car.

Another conversation you can have with your kids is to reveal your past money mistakes. It's good for them to hear things you wish you had done differently. Don't be ashamed of your past. See it as a learning experience and a way to show them how to avoid the same pain you experienced.

A good rule of thumb is to "share, but don't scare." Don't try to explain the concept of foreclosure to your six-year-old. This will only scare them, and they may end up waking you up later that night because they had a nightmare of a banker trying to kick them out of their house! Instead, make these conversations age-appropriate. Sharing your stories with them will go further than you realize. My parents have always been open with their story of bankruptcy and debt. Because of that, I learned to stay away from the life-restricting obligation of debt. I'm thankful they were honest with us and didn't try to sweep things under the rug and act like everything was perfect.

This was a quick flyover of how to help your children understand how money works, but if you are looking for a more in-depth resource on this topic, my dad and I wrote a book together called *Smart Money Smart Kids* that hits every aspect of raising money-smart children. If you have kids and want to set them up to win with money, you should check it out.

Adult Kids, Talk to Your Parents

Grown kids need to talk to their parents about money too. This can be difficult, but it still needs to be done in certain situations. There is a whole generation of older parents who don't have the means for retirement, don't have a plan in place for when they pass, and don't know how they're going to handle many of the "golden years" decisions.

I've heard too many tragic stories about fathers who passed away without life insurance, mothers who didn't have long-term care insurance, and parents who died without wills. None of these people saw these tragedies coming. People want to think their family members have more time, so they avoid these difficult conversations. Don't let this happen to you! Initiate these conversations before the need arises.

As a grown child, you need to talk to your parents about their future financial plans. Be sure they have a will in place, get the facts around their insurance situation, and review any other related details while there is time for a course correction, if needed. You don't have to know all the details within each of those categories; you just want to be sure they have a plan in place. Whatever they haven't addressed may eventually become your responsibility, so go ahead and ask about these things as soon as possible.

These can be awkward conversations, but they will help you eliminate a great deal of stress *when* (not *if*) your family member dies. And it will give you the time and space to grieve.

You're trying to take charge of your money in order to win in the long term. You want your parents in that place too. Again, you don't have to know all the information that's in their will if they aren't comfortable sharing those details. However, it's wise to get a plan in place to ensure that their house is in order when the time comes.

DEFINE THE RELATIONSHIP

There's a special conversation, commonly known as the DTR, that marks a turning point in a dating relationship. DTR stands for "define the relationship." The conversation signals a change in commitment or focus when the relationship starts to get serious. This talk is usually awkward and sometimes doesn't turn out exactly how you expect, but it's a key milestone in a growing relationship.

Talking about money can also be one of those DTR moments in a relationship. Your willingness to approach the subject with honesty and vulnerability with your spouse or fiancé, parents, boyfriend or girlfriend, and children is critical to winning with money. You'll never know if you are living life in alignment with your core values, dreams, and beliefs until you have honest conversations around those things.

Winston and I don't talk about money because we *have* to, but because we *want* to. The conversation always starts with dollars and cents, but it ends with dreams, possibilities, and opportunities. A big part of marriage is creating a life you love together; money is simply a tool to help you realize those dreams.

Granted, money isn't always easy to talk about. But if you're willing to endure the occasional discomfort and awkwardness those conversations bring, you'll find the freedom to love each other more deeply and with greater satisfaction than you thought possible. Why? *Because you'll be on the same page.* That is what will pull you through the darkest days and the brightest moments of your life.

— Habit 5 —

Save Like You Mean It

10

Saving for Life

Mom is going to be so proud of me! That's what I was thinking as I walked into the post office. Since I was young, she has drilled into my head the practice of sending handwritten thank-you notes whenever you receive a gift. The fact that I was mailing out *all* of my thank-you notes for my wedding gifts just thirty days after our wedding was a huge deal for me.

One thing Winston and I didn't cut back on when it came to our wedding was the guest list. So, consequently, we had hundreds of thank-you notes to write, seal, stamp, and mail. When I finished the last one, I couldn't wait to mail them and check this monumental project off my list. I proudly carried those thank-you notes in a big box and handed them over to the nice gentleman behind the counter at the post office. I felt like I could conquer the world as I walked out of there that day.

I put my car in drive and started to slowly pull forward out of my parking space when I heard the sound of metal. My heart sank as I thought, *Wait! What is that?* I wasn't supposed to be hearing scraping and crunching. I wondered where it was coming from. I stopped and looked in the direction of the sound, where an elderly man stood with a look of horror on his face. His expression told me all I needed to know—I had hit his car.

Whatever feeling of accomplishment I had about the thank-you notes vanished as I got out and walked around my car to see what I had done. I was mortified and apologized immediately. This wasn't just a dent in his car door. The door was bending in the opposite direction.

The good news was that no one got hurt and we had insurance. The bad news was that our deductible was $1,000—and that was a lot of money for us. At the time, we were young newlyweds who had only been married for thirty days. If we hadn't had some money saved for moments just like this, a bad situation could have quickly become much, much worse.

LIFE IS FULL OF SURPRISES

You never know when life is going to happen to you. The washer will go out, the hot water heater will break, or the unexpected medical bill will come. Choosing to save for these moments won't prevent them from happening, but the habit will give you confidence and options when they do.

Next Month Never Comes

Saving money is something we know we *should* do, like going to the dentist every six months, visiting the doctor annually, exercising, and eating right. But like with those things, we sometimes fudge when it comes to actually doing them. It's easy to talk ourselves into saving *next* month. The only problem is that "next month" never comes. It just keeps getting pushed out another month.

Saving—even a small amount—will give you peace of mind. The habit will give you a sense that you're doing small things now that will give you a big benefit when you need to (legitimately) dip into it. The disciplined practice of taking money from your paycheck and putting it away for the future is hard sometimes, but you'll be surprised how quickly your savings can grow if you're consistent. Like the Bible says, "Wealth gained hastily will dwindle, but whoever gathers little by little will increase it" (Proverbs 13:11 ESV).

Today vs. Tomorrow

There are so many things pulling at us in the present. The practice of saving for the future can seem impossible and, frankly, not much fun. For me, *spending* money feels far more exciting! When you buy things you want and need today, you get that feeling of instant gratification. There's no waiting.

However, having nothing in savings adds to the stress level in the middle of a crisis. You will be forced to use debt to bridge the gap—and that debt will only compound your problem. Using debt for a car repair leaves you with a car problem *and* a money problem. The same is true for any unexpected event when we have no financial margin. When we don't have any money saved, we are cautiously looking around each corner, expecting something to jump out and ruin our day. That's a miserable way to live.

When it comes to saving money, there are many things we could talk about. For now, let's focus on two important areas: building an emergency fund and preparing for stage-of-life events.

THE EMERGENCY FUND

You can't schedule emergencies, but you can count on the fact that you will have them. You don't know *when* they're coming; you just know they will . . . someday. That's why it's important to prepare now so you'll be ready.

The emergency fund is a *must* in life. This is your safety net or cushion between you and the inevitable. The fund is there to catch you and make the fall a little less painful. Begin with a $1,000 emergency fund. As fast as you can, get this little starter emergency fund in place.

Saving $1,000 can feel impossible if you're starting with nothing. However, most people can "find" money when they want to buy or do something that is important to them. If you're already strapped for cash, consider selling some stuff online, skipping the restaurants for a month or two, or cutting out some extra entertainment like concerts, movies, and events. You may even take on a part-time job if necessary to get you to the $1,000 mark.

Do whatever you have to do to get to this point as quickly as possible. Chances are, $1,000 is enough to keep you from turning to debt when the unexpected happens. Sure there are emergencies that will require more than that, but this will give you a great start. Besides, having only $1,000 in the bank for emergencies isn't the long-term plan. Once you are debt-free except for your mortgage, bump your starter emergency fund up to three to six months' worth of expenses. That will be your fully funded emergency fund.

Can you imagine having no debt payments and six months' worth of expenses saved in the bank? Seriously, stop and think about what life would feel like at that point. And the great thing is, you can do it! I hear stories every day from people just like you who have reached this goal. This financial goal is a life-changer, and I promise you can get there.

Reasons Why

The emergency fund will help with all the difficult and unexpected things that happen in life. The money is there to help you navigate a job loss, replace your heating and air unit, fix your car, and cover unexpected doctor bills. This last one is serious. Medical debt is consistently one of the leading causes of bankruptcy in America today. Having any cash on hand to help with those expenses is important, even if what you have saved only covers deductibles and co-pays.

I have counseled people who were able to overcome impossible odds because those funds were there. And it's not just about the money sitting in the bank; it's about the power the emergency fund gives you in a crisis. It enables you to act—or at least *react*—without going into a panic or falling back into debt. When you have cash saved and the unexpected happens, you have the power to focus on what's really important—a sick child or a tree branch sticking through your roof—instead of focusing on money.

Keep It Separate

Your emergency fund needs to be in a separate account from your regularly budgeted spending money. If it just sits in your checking account, it will be difficult to know if you're unintentionally using "emergency" dollars for everyday purchases. But while it's in a separate account, it still needs to be in a place where you can get to it when you need it, any time, any day. That's why a basic savings account or a money market account with online, ATM, and debit-card access is the best plan. That way you can act immediately, whether or not the bank's open at the time.

You or your spouse may struggle with the idea of putting $10,000 or so in a basic savings account or a money market account that doesn't earn much interest. I get that, but you need to think of the emergency fund as *insurance*, not an *investment*. And insurance *costs* you money, right? Don't get fancy with this money, trying to find the best rate of return. That's not why it's there. It's tucked away for emergencies. It won't earn much, but when you need it, you'll be glad you have it.

I can't begin to tell you the peace that I felt once we fully funded our emergency fund. Now, when I look online at our accounts, I don't even include the emergency fund amount when I add up what we have in savings. I emotionally don't want to think about it because I never want to be tempted to spend it. I want to avoid using that money so much, in fact, that I want to have an emergency fund for our emergency fund!

STAGE-OF-LIFE EVENTS

Emergencies aren't the only thing you want to plan for. There are also expected stage-of-life events. The sooner you begin putting money away for these things, the more prepared you'll be when it's time to pay for them.

So what are we talking about here? Think of the big purchases or occasions in the future that will cost a lot of money. I'm talking about buying a car, getting married, taking a big anniversary vacation, or sending your kids to college. These things aren't emergencies, but they can be incredibly expensive. With the emergency fund, you know you'll need money for *something* at *some time*, you just don't know what or when. With stage-of-life events, you pretty much know *what's* coming, *when* it's coming, and *how much* it'll cost. That means there's no excuse for not being prepared!

Let's talk about a few of the big ones that trip up a lot of people.

Saving for a Car

Most people want a great vehicle. I get it. You don't want to drive around in something you aren't proud of or that feels like it's going to break down every time you drive it. Neither do I. We all want to drive a car we love and feel is safe and reliable. So with that in mind, we just need a plan to get us there.

Rule number one—and we talked about this in Chapter Four—is to never even consider getting a car loan. Making payments on a car is the fast track to financial mediocrity. A car goes down in value the second you drive it off the lot, but your payments are based on what it was worth while it was sitting in the showroom with five miles on the odometer. That means a few years later, you're still paying the brand-new car price even though the vehicle is worth half (or less) of that. Paying interest on something that is worth less and less every month is a terrible idea no matter how much money you have.

I have talked to so many people over the years who shrug this off and say, "Oh, come on, Rachel. I'm always going to have a car payment, so I might as well have a nice car, right?" Wrong. Few things will keep you as broke over the course of your life as surrendering to the eternal car payment. The routine of making car payments every single month of your entire adult life is one of the worst financial habits I can think of and one of the first bad habits you need to break. Most people have been doing this for so long that they can't even imagine a life without car payments. But if you want to live the life you've always dreamed of living, you've got to break the car-payment habit and replace it with a habit of saving.

One of my favorite *Saturday Night Live* skits shows a financial counselor trying to convince Steve Martin to save up and pay for things using cash instead of debt. My favorite line in the routine is when Steve Martin looks up at the guy with a confused look on his face and asks, "But where do you get this 'saved' money?" It's hilarious and pokes fun at our debt-obsessed culture. But there's a lot of truth hidden in the humor. "Where do I get this 'saved' money?" is a question a lot of people are asking these days. So let's look at how you can do this for your next car purchase.

Let's say you're driving a car that's worth about $8,000 today, and you will probably replace that car this time next year. For the next twelve months, try to save $500 every month. That means you will have $6,000 a year from now. At that point, you could probably sell your car for around $7,000. Then you'd have the cash to go buy a great $13,000 car. Keep following that same formula over and over for the rest of your life. You could keep doing this and upgrade your car as often as you wanted to, and you'd still never have a car payment again!

I can hear it now: "Yeah, Rachel, that sounds great . . . if I had an extra $500 a month laying around." The thing is, though, every day people commit to spending $500 a month on their cars. Believe it or not, the average car payment in America today is nearly $500.[1] Why is it that nobody thinks they can *save* $500 a month, but everybody thinks they can *afford* a $500 payment each month? It's because they've bought the lie that they'll always have a car payment. If you can make that mental shift, if you can break the habit of car payments, you can free up literally millions of dollars in potential retirement income. This is a big, big deal.

If you have a car payment currently, then you either need to pay it off with the debt snowball or sell it. If you owe more on it than it's worth, you could sell it and take out a small loan for the difference. At that point you will just buy a cheap, reliable car with cash and start the savings plan from there. That's assuming you don't have any other debts, of course. If you have more debts than just your car, you need to drive your "new" used car for a while as you clean up your debt. Then, once you're debt-free with a full emergency fund, you can start saving up for a newer car.

This may mean that you have to drive an older, $1,000 car around for a while. I know that sounds terrible, but it's just temporary. If driving a twenty-year-old Camry for a year or so now will enable you to drive whatever you want in the near future, it's worth it!

Make saving for a car a new habit, even if you don't need a new car today. We all know we will need to replace our cars at some point. Depending on how much you drive, you may replace cars more frequently than other people. Add a new line item to your budget so you can start saving money in a car fund.

Saving for Retirement

One of the biggest stage-of-life events is retirement. It's something that many people have a hard time wrapping their minds around simply because it's so far into the future, especially for young adults or families with little kids running around.

However, the data on retirement savings is sobering. Studies show that one-third of people in their thirties and forties have nothing saved for retirement, and almost seven out of ten people in their twenties haven't saved a dime yet.[2] That's crazy! Investing in those early years is your best chance to build lasting wealth over the course of your life, but 70 percent of people in their twenties don't think it's a big deal! And a third of the people hitting mid-life haven't even started yet! No, no, no. I don't care how old you are, you have to make retirement savings a priority and a habit—even if it doesn't feel urgent today.

If you're overwhelmed by the thought of saving for retirement, know that you're not alone. I'll let you in on a secret that's not so secret—saving for retirement is possible. Your ability to feel confident about your retirement years depends upon your willingness to develop a new money habit of saving like you mean it. If you need help with this, I recommend you check out my favorite book on retirement planning, *Retire Inspired*, by my friend Chris Hogan.

Saying No Today Is Hard

The discipline of saying no to something in the present so you can focus on something thirty or forty years in the future won't seem fun. I'm right there with you. I'm a spender, remember? Setting that money aside for the future is tough! But guess what? I know that the older, retirement-aged version of myself will be a spender too. And the only money Future Rachel will have to spend is the money I send her way today. And if I do it right, Future Rachel will have more to spend than Current Rachel would know what to do with! But that will only happen if I commit to a lifelong habit of saving.

P. T. Barnum once said, "You will find there is more satisfaction in rational saving than in irrational spending." The only problem is, you may not feel that satisfaction in the moment. I had a pretty good reminder of this when I was pregnant. I had been working like crazy at the time, and my commission check showed it. It was a great feeling, but I was absolutely exhausted. During that week's regular budget conversation, I told Winston the amount I was expecting for that check, and I admitted that I was already dreaming of what we'd be able to get for the nursery with that month's extra income.

But then reality sank in. I remembered that a few months earlier during another conversation, Winston and I had agreed on a big money goal for the year. We both wanted to focus on our retirement savings that year, so we decided that any extra money we got throughout the year would go straight into our retirement accounts until we maxed them out for the year.

Shortly after we made that decision together, Winston had a great month at work and was expecting a pretty nice paycheck. He mentioned wanting to buy some new hunting gear, but we talked about it and I reminded him about our retirement goal for the year. He agreed, and that extra money went to our retirement instead of to Bass Pro Shop. He was disappointed, but it was a decision we had made together months earlier. We were just sticking to the plan.

But now, with my big commission check on the way, the tables had turned. When I brought up the extra nursery stuff I wanted, it was his turn to remind me of our retirement goal. Can you just imagine having this conversation with an emotional, pregnant woman? Yeah . . . not fun. Poor guy. I have to admit, I was really disappointed. Okay, fine—I was mad. In the moment it seemed so annoying to put money away that I wouldn't see for decades. I mean, the precious baby growing inside me deserved a beautiful brass crib, not the cheap wooden one we had just bought. Oh, the hormones were taking over! However, when I came back to reality, I really couldn't argue. He wasn't being cheap or mean; he was just reminding me of our shared goals. It was a decision we had made together to focus on long-term saving, and we were holding each other accountable. That's how marriage works!

Now, could I have spent *some* of that paycheck on the nursery? Sure. We could have talked about it and maybe carved out a little chunk of that paycheck for extra nursery stuff. But here's the thing: we didn't need to. We had already budgeted what we were going to spend on the nursery, and I didn't need to add any more money to the budget. The fact that I was getting a little extra money on one paycheck didn't mean our nursery or retirement plans had to change. It's not that I was saying no to ever spending money on our new baby or that Winston could never buy new hunting stuff again. It was just that any extra money that year was allocated to something we had already agreed on.

Having the discipline to say no to something in the present so we could focus on retirement was hard. It was a huge reality check for me, in fact. But now, looking back at that moment, I know we made the right decision. After living with a baby for a while now, I know the nursery really isn't that important as long as there is a crib and a comfy chair. Our retirement accounts, though, are looking solid. No hunting gear or nursery décor could make up for the extra tens or hundreds of thousands of dollars we'll enjoy at retirement because of those two tough, in-the-moment decisions in our twenties.

When Are You Ready to Save for Retirement?

Retirement planning has to be a priority for you, regardless of your age, but you need to make sure you're *ready* to start saving for retirement before you dive in. Retirement savings should enter your financial plan once you are debt-free except for the house and you have a fully funded emergency fund of three to six months' worth of expenses in the bank. Once you get there, you're ready to start climbing the retirement mountain.

I often get pushback on this point from people—usually the serious planners and savers—who want to prioritize retirement above anything else in their budget. If you are up to your neck in debt and have no savings, but you do have a lot of money tucked away in your 401(k), what do you think will happen in an emergency? You'll either go deeper into debt (bad plan), or you'll go to the one place you actually do have some money: your 401(k). That's a bad plan too. Borrowing against your 401(k) robs you of that money's earning power and basically puts you in debt to yourself. And outright withdrawing funds from your 401(k) early will cost you about 40 percent of your money in taxes and penalties. Make sure you have a strong financial foundation by being debt-free with a fully funded emergency fund before you start saving for retirement.

When you're ready to start saving for retirement, you should put 15 percent of your income into tax-favored retirement plans. "Tax favored" simply means you're taking advantage of some great investing vehicles that provide some protection against taxes eating up all of your savings when you hit retirement. Staying at 15 percent for a while is a great balance. It still leaves you with enough income to enjoy life and work on paying off your house early, but it's also a significant enough contribution every month that your retirement accounts will start to grow quickly.

There are a million rules and details when it comes to investing, so you always want to work with an investment professional you trust. Make sure it's someone who has the heart of a teacher. This person should explain to you, in layman's terms, how these investments work. If you don't understand how something works, don't invest your money in it. If your financial pro gets impatient with you or starts talking down to you, then fire him or her and find someone who will respectfully walk you through the steps. Don't blindly take someone else's word on what you should or shouldn't do with your money.

I know this was all a pretty light touch on the huge and complicated world of investing. For a full understanding of the ins and outs of retirement planning, again, you should pick up a copy of *Retire Inspired* by Chris Hogan. It's pretty much the only retirement book I've seen that's easy to understand and actually fun to read.

Saving for College

If you have kids, the next step after building momentum with your retirement savings is to start saving for their college education. Yes, this means you will fund your retirement *before* funding your kid's college. I've talked to *many* parents who disagree. They can't even imagine putting money away for themselves before helping their kids with college. However, the reality is that retirement is going to happen whether you like it or not, and your kids may *not* go to college. Your kids will have many opportunities to help pay for college themselves, but no one is going to sweep in and cover your retirement. That's up to you.

So how do you make the most of the time you have before the kids head to college? First, take advantage of tax-favored savings options. One type is the ESA (Education Savings Account), which grows tax-free as long as you use that money for school. If you don't meet the income requirements for an ESA, check out the 529 plans available. Those are similar to the ESA, but they come with some different options—some good, some bad. For example, you should only consider 529 plans that leave you in control of the investment and don't automatically adjust based on the age of your child. Just like with retirement planning, I recommend you get personal, professional help from a financial professional you trust when it comes to college planning.

You want to take advantage of all the time you have before your kids head off to school, so start early. That said, don't beat yourself up if you honestly can't afford to put anything away for college after investing 15 percent of your income for your own retirement. Helping cover their tuition isn't something they are entitled to; it's a blessing. If you can help your kids, great! If you can't, that's okay. It doesn't make you a bad parent.

Don't forget that your child will have plenty of opportunities to pay their tuition, including working and applying for scholarships. Some parents act like expecting a student to work while in college is the worst thing in the world, but it's not. Having a job teaches responsibility, time management, and the pride that comes from accomplishing something huge. In addition, an unbelievable amount of money is available to students in the form of scholarships. All it takes is filling out an application and sometimes writing a short essay!

Of all the college payment options available to your children, student loans should *not* be one of them. We're in the middle of a student loan crisis that is crippling an entire generation of recent graduates. These young adults are leaving college with an average $35,000 in student loans—before they ever even get their first job![3]

My advice is simple: Your kids need to go to a school they can afford. Don't worry about what school your friends are sending their kids to. Other families shouldn't play a part in this decision. You need to do what's best for *your* family, not theirs.

College planning is so important that I dedicated a whole chapter to this one subject in my book *Smart Money Smart Kids*. If you've got kids at home, it's worth it to dig deeper into the ins and outs of paying for college.

Saving for a Wedding

When we think of milestones in life that could potentially cost a lot of money, weddings are often at the top of that list. Maybe you're single and plan on getting married someday. Or maybe you're a parent and already thinking ahead to your child's wedding. If you have a daughter (or more than one), traditionally, you will help pay for the wedding. You're not a bad parent if you can't help with this, but if you're able to, that's great. If you have a son, traditionally, the rehearsal dinner is on you, but again, only if you can afford it.

When it comes to weddings, it's easy to go crazy, but that doesn't mean you should. This is an industry that will try to convince you to spend as much money as you could possibly imagine. The average wedding in the United States costs a whopping $28,000—and that doesn't include the engagement ring, rehearsal dinner, or honeymoon.[4]

At the end of the day, your adult child will be married, whether that is in a nearby municipal park or in a Park Avenue hotel in the middle of Manhattan. Remember, keep the comparisons out and keep the wedding, rehearsal dinner, and honeymoon in perspective, and be sure to prioritize how you save for the big day in light of some of the more pressing areas we've been talking about.

Saving for a Growing Family

Many young couples say things like, "Sure, we want kids, but we just can't afford to be parents right now." Kids can be expensive! However, if you can enter parenthood with money in the bank and no debt, it'll definitely be easier to handle any little surprises that may pop up with your bundle of joy.

Be careful here, however. Money should not be the deciding

factor in whether or not you're ready to have children. If you wait until you have "enough money" to have kids, you may never have them. If you and your spouse are ready emotionally, then don't let money—or even debt—get in your way.

Of course, you don't want to go *deeper* in debt, so you'll need to budget everything carefully. If you're currently working on your debt snowball, you should stop making extra payments on your debt while you're expecting so you can save up a pile of money. Then, once the baby is home safe and you're clear of any birth-related surprises, you can throw that extra money at your debt and get back to your snowball.

Deciding to have a child can't be an excuse to go nuts and throw your financial plan out the window. Instead, bringing kids into the picture just makes budgeting, saving, and planning even more important. After all, the stakes are a lot higher when you're responsible for someone else!

Saving for Celebration Trips

The only thing better than a great vacation is a vacation celebrating something! Trips are so much more special when the purpose is to celebrate a birthday, holiday, or, best of all, a wedding anniversary. If you value travel in your life, celebration trips can be some of the best money you'll ever spend.

When our five-year anniversary came around, I was five months pregnant. We knew this would be our last big, carefree getaway for a while, and we wanted to make it special. Since our wedding anniversary couldn't exactly sneak up on us, we had planned how much money we'd need for the trip. Our anniversary was in December, and we started saving in June. We planned every detail as we saved for those six months, and the trip was amazing. As great as the trip was, though, I think the best part was that we were able to bring home only memories and pictures—and no credit card debt. You'll enjoy those getaways so much more when they don't come back to haunt your mailbox a month later.

STARTING THE SAVING HABIT

Developing a habit of saving money doesn't just happen on its own. Many people never get started because they are so focused on their present needs, and planning far into the future seems too daunting. But the actual *discipline* of saving is more important than *how much* you save in the beginning. You *can* start saving something today, even if it's only the change in your pocket.

If you're living paycheck to paycheck right now, then it's important to prioritize your savings. Otherwise, you'll burn out trying to save for everything we talked about in this chapter. Begin with your starter emergency fund and build from there.

If you're out of debt and living on a budget, then you should be able to focus on big savings goals like your emergency fund, retirement, a special celebration vacation, or anything else that you want to do down the road. The goal here is to do and have the things you value in life. Some of those things come with bigger price tags, so you just have to be a little more intentional (and patient) when saving for them.

11

The Biggest Savings Goal of Your Life

My dad loves real estate. When I was growing up, our whole family would pile in the car after church on Sundays and "go for a drive"—which meant we were going to drive slowly through neighborhoods and look at houses. The most exciting part was if there was a house being built, we would all get out of the car to walk through it (if it was safe to do so). Houses became events and experiences for me. They were something to look at on beautiful Sunday afternoons. But now, as an adult, I understand how much responsibility comes with owning a home.

Whatever season of life you're in, buying and owning a house can be a game changer. Maybe you just got married and want to move into the home you always dreamed of living in as newlyweds. Maybe your kids are about to start school and you're looking for a home in the best school system. Maybe you're single and ready to move into something more permanent.

One thing that puts many homebuyers into bad situations is rushing into a purchase without taking the time to get all the facts. There are so many places in this process where our emotions can take over. We either downplay or outright ignore that little voice in our heads that knows better. Or worse, we think we can outsmart the system. The numbers might seem high for our personal budget, but we think we can find a way to make it work. We make a huge purchase in spite of the risk because we've convinced ourselves it's the *perfect* house.

Then trouble starts to creep in. The "newlywed" phase passes, and the roof starts leaking, the furnace breaks, and the dishwasher needs replacing. The monthly mortgage payment is now catching up to us. The whole thing suddenly seems to be a big mistake—all because we wanted a particular house and wouldn't consider any other options.

When you are in a place you don't want to be, any amount of time feels like an eternity. That is the place many people find themselves after making a bad housing decision. Let's not allow that to happen. There are some steps to take in home buying that will guarantee a wise purchase and ensure the purchase of your home will be a blessing, not a curse. These steps will make you slow down, look for the best deal, and perhaps save a little longer. In the end you will be in a great place financially and you'll be ready to buy the right home at the right time.

You might be wondering why we're talking about buying a house in a chapter about saving. Shouldn't this fall under spending instead? Well . . . yes and no. Sure, a house is something you *purchase*, so it's definitely something you *spend* money on. But before you sit down at a closing table, you need to save for a long time. Saving up for a house—even if it's a big down payment—can be the biggest saving goal you ever face. And, once you're a homeowner, your house will probably be the biggest, long-term investment you have. Every dollar you spend on a mortgage or down payment is like putting money in a house-sized piggy bank, so it makes sense to look at home buying through the lens of saving.

A BLESSING OR A CURSE?

Buying and moving into a home can be such an exciting time in life. It represents a shift in our goals and the commitment it takes to reach them. Like I said before, a house is the biggest investment most people ever make—and with it comes a lot of excitement, anxiety, responsibility, and opportunity. If you do it right, it can be one of the biggest blessings of your life. If you do it wrong, it can become a weight around your neck, dragging you down for decades.

Buying a Lie

Sadly, I've heard as many horror stories as success stories from people when they talk about their home decisions. There's so much emotion and pressure tied into most of these buying decisions that it's easy to make a mistake or an impulse decision that you come to regret. You can get so focused on the *look* of a certain home that you *overlook* problems with the foundation or plumbing. A friend moves into a high-end neighborhood that's outside your price range, but you feel pressured to move there yourself. You fall in love with a house and scramble for ways to justify paying more than you should. You're determined to put your kids in a particular school system because you want them to have "the best," even if it makes zero financial sense for your family. You get house fever just because you saw a friend's new house on Facebook. Any of that sound familiar?

Then, once you're in too deep to see clearly, with visions of the "perfect home" clouding your judgment, you rush into a bad thirty-year mortgage that costs you tens of thousands of dollars in interest payments, fifteen years of extra, unnecessary debt, and three decades of monthly stress and anxiety. The payments you thought you could afford end up overshadowing the excitement you felt on moving day. All of these issues and more hit unsuspecting home-buyers in the face every day.

I want you to be prepared to buy your next home the right way. We're going to talk about how much of a down payment you should put down, what kind of mortgage to take out, and pitfalls to avoid. If you take the time to learn all of this now, you will become a pre-pared homebuyer.

The Best Way to Buy

When it comes to buying a home, money shouldn't be the *only* factor to consider—but it should be high on the list. That doesn't mean you should buy an unsuitable home because it's cheap. I know people who have made this mistake, thinking they were being financially responsible, but the move ended up costing them a for-tune in repairs and lost resale value. Knowing how much you can afford is essential, but it's only part of the equation. You also need to factor in how much space you'll need, what kind of commute works best for you, and how close you want to be to friends and family.

When it comes to purchasing a home, the absolute best option is the 100 percent down plan. Not 100 percent *financing*; 100 per-cent *down*. That's right: paying cash is the best way to buy a home. Now before you think I've completely lost my mind, consider this: What if you never had a house payment? What if mortgage debt was not part of your present or your future? What if buying a home never included a trip to a mortgage broker?

It may sound crazy to you, but this is a legitimate option. Almost 25 percent of all homes purchased in the last fifteen years were bought with cash![1] I've heard some pretty amazing stories from people about paying cash for homes. One couple lived above an elderly woman's garage for free because the husband did her yard work. They lived there for five years, banked his $50,000 salary, and only lived off her teacher's salary. After four years—at age twenty-seven—they paid cash for a $150,000 home and had thousands of dollars in savings to furnish it! While that's an incredible story, it's not as uncommon as you might think.

Another couple lived inexpensively for five years while all their friends were running out and buying houses. They recently wrote a check to fully purchase their townhome. Another couple inherited some money from a grandfather. Instead of using that money as a down payment, they chose to put that inheritance with their savings to pay cash for a smaller house—free and clear.

This is a real option, but it means you might not buy the same kind of home in the same kind of neighborhood as your friends. If you value a nicer home in a nicer neighborhood, then let's talk about how to buy it reasonably. If you value the freedom and peace that comes with never owing a bank a dime for your home, then make a plan to get it done. Dream and think big for yourself, your family, and your future. Don't worry about what your friends have or how big their houses are. You aren't living their lives. You're living your own life, so make it a life you love.

THE MORTGAGE LANDSCAPE

If you do take out a mortgage, do it the right way. There are a million mortgage options out there, and unfortunately most of them are pretty bad options. Take some time to learn the basics when it comes to mortgages. Don't simply trust what a banker is trying to sell you. Understand your options and pick the one that's right for you, not for the bank or broker.

I have a friend who made pretty much every mistake possible

when buying his first home. He didn't know what he was doing, and he didn't get any advice from someone who knew the real estate world. The house and neighborhood they chose were reasonable for their income, but reason went out the window when it came to the mortgage. This otherwise intelligent guy blindly followed the lender's advice and ended up with an 80/20, interest-only loan with nothing down and variable interest rates on both loans! He paid his monthly payment for years, never knowing what the interest rate would be, and never earning a dime in equity. This was a nightmare scenario, and it's only by the grace of God that he got out of that house before it wrecked his entire financial future.

My friend isn't dumb; he was just uninformed. He honestly didn't know any better. I never want you to go into something as monumental as getting a mortgage without knowing what you're doing, so let's cover the basics.

Ignorance Is Not Bliss

Ignorance is not bliss when it comes to mortgages. A bad decision could cost you tens of thousands of dollars or more, so educate yourself. Learn the language and best practices of home buying. It doesn't have to be intimidating; it's not that much different than getting into a new hobby.

When you were learning about sports for the first time, you heard terms like *offense, defense, play clock,* and *out of bounds.* If you enter the programming world, you will hear terms like *code, front-end developer,* and *implementation.* In the mortgage world you're going to hear terms like *down payment, rate, conventional, balloon, fixed,* and *adjustable*—just to name a few. Don't be intimidated by all the jargon. I can break all of this down into one simple rule of thumb. Write this down. Learn it. Live by it. When it's time to buy a house, pull this rule back out and make sure you stick to it.

Here it is: when it's time to shop around for a mortgage, go for a fifteen-year, fixed-rate mortgage with at least 10 percent down and a monthly payment of no more than 25 percent of your take-home pay.

Yes, that's a mouthful, so let's break it down into a few pieces so you can better understand each part of that rule.

Fifteen-Year, Fixed-Rate Loan

A fifteen-year loan will get you out of debt fifteen years sooner than a thirty-year loan. Shocking, I know. Becoming and staying totally debt-free as quickly as possible should always be the goal. Many homebuyers simply sign up for a thirty-year home loan like it's their only option. It has become a default loan term because it offers a *slightly* lower monthly payment. That kind of short-term thinking will keep you in debt for the rest of your life. With homes, cars, and anything else, you should ask, "How much?" instead of "How much per month?" The few hundred bucks you may save each month on that mortgage payment will cost you tens or hundreds of thousands of dollars in unnecessary interest payments over the course of thirty years.

And don't tell yourself that you'll take out a thirty-year loan but pay it off in fifteen years. This might sound like a smart plan, but it rarely works out like you expect it to. Something else will always seem more important each month, so all those extra payments you thought you'd make will end up going to vacations, extra restaurant meals, and the kids' sports fees.

If you *plan* on paying it off in fifteen years and *want* to pay it off in fifteen years, choose a fifteen-year, fixed-rate mortgage. If you can't pay it off in fifteen years, you're trying to buy more house than you can afford. You either need to save a bigger down payment or lower your expectations to better match your financial reality.

10 to 20 Percent Down

Speaking of down payments, you should put *at least* 10 percent down on your home. If you can put 20 percent down, you will avoid something called Private Mortgage Insurance (PMI), which is paid to the lender for securities that are necessary when taking out a mortgage. If you can avoid PMI, you should—it's extra money you don't need to spend.

If you put down less than 20 percent initially, be sure to keep an eye on your loan-to-value ratio as you start to make payments. That basically means how much of your home's value you *own* versus how much of your home's value you *owe*. Once you've paid off 20 percent or more of your home's value, you can have the bank drop the PMI. Don't trust the bank to do this automatically. You must watch for it yourself and alert the bank if necessary.

Monthly Payment No More than 25 Percent of Your Take-Home Pay

When it comes to your monthly payment, you don't want it to be more than 25 percent of your take-home pay. This may sound conservative, but if it's any more than that, you'll have too much of your income going back out the door in the form of mortgage payments. That's when you become what's called "house poor."

I spoke with a woman after an event in San Antonio who told me her mortgage payment was close to 50 percent of her family's take-home pay. The monthly obligation was such a point of stress for her. She said she felt like they could never have any traction with their money because of their large monthly mortgage payment.

Later she emailed an update to her situation. They moved because of her husband's job and decided to purchase a smaller house with a lower monthly payment. She said it felt like she could breathe again. She was still able to live in a wonderful home, but it wasn't pulling all of their hard-earned money out of their hands. She realized that she valued the peace of mind that came with a reasonable mortgage more than she valued the impressive-looking appearance of her old home. I don't blame her! I'd choose peace any and every day over stress and worry.

Now, one important thing to note when calculating your monthly payment: remember to include PMI (if applicable), property taxes, homeowner's insurance premiums, and homeowner's association (HOA) fees. Sometimes HOAs are rolled into the payment but not always. Depending on where you live, you could find yourself looking at an extra $100 or more a month just in HOA fees. Know what you're getting into before you buy.

THE RIGHT TIME TO BUY

I hear people talk about the housing market all the time, usually as a justification for buying a house they can't afford. "But Rachel, it's a buyer's market! We'd be crazy not to take advantage of these prices and low interest rates!"

The hard truth I share with these hopeful buyers is that, if you're not personally ready to buy, it doesn't matter what the housing market is doing. You don't want the market driving your decisions; you want to drive your own decisions. Sure, you want to take advantage of great home prices and lower interest rates when you can, but that should only be when you're already financially ready to buy.

When Are You Ready?

So what makes you ready to buy a home? First, you need to be out of debt and have a fully funded emergency fund of three to six months of expenses. If you have two car payments, credit card debt, student loans, and no savings, buying a home will drive your stress levels through the roof. There's no chance of that house being a blessing if you're pulling your hair out trying to make the payment every month.

And, yes, I know you're probably going to have to pay some rent if you aren't paying a mortgage, but it's still worth it. Owning a home increases your risk. There's no landlord to call when the roof starts leaking or the HVAC goes out. You'll be on the hook for a world of new expenses from the first day of owning that "perfect" home. The truth is, it's only perfect if it doesn't break your financial back, and that's exactly what'll happen if you're already overloaded with other debts.

Second, you need to have a solid down payment of at least 10 percent (but 20 percent is better). This down payment needs to be completely separate from your emergency fund. Never leave your emergency savings at the closing table. Buying a house introduces a whole new world of potential emergencies, and your emergency fund needs to be in place to protect you.

Third, you need to be ready to take on a payment of no more than 25 percent of your take-home pay on a fifteen-year, fixed-rate loan. We've already talked about this, but I'm serious. Do several mock monthly budgets based on the new loan amount. Be realistic too. Don't cut your budget to the bone just to make the numbers work on paper. We all know that's not how life works!

If you have all of these things going for you and your family is ready for a move, then you can take the leap knowing you're making a wise choice.

If you aren't where you need to be with these three things, you may have to put home ownership off for a year or two until you get to a place where buying a home is a blessing and not a curse. This may not be in your ideal timeline, but if you temporarily put off your feelings and emotions and approach home buying in a smart way, then the next ten to fifteen years are going to come with far less worry and stress—all because you've lowered your risk.

I don't want to be a Debbie Downer, because owning a home is so exciting. However, I want you to do it wisely. By doing things a little more slowly than most people would, you will love the life you have set up for yourself because stress and worry won't be part of the equation.

When Not to Buy

While I'm a fan of home ownership, there are times when I would suggest not owning a home. One of those times is when you are between the ages of eighteen and twenty-two (or college-age). The last thing a nineteen-year-old needs to worry about is a mortgage payment and property taxes. Don't put that burden on yourself at this time in your life. Instead, this is the time to rent, rent, rent. You'll be past this phase of life in four to five years at most. That's not enough time to own a home and get the investment out of it.

Now, for those overachieving college students who do make a good income while in school, it might seem like a good idea to buy a home instead of "throwing your money away" on rent. Slow down. Your college years and the few years right after graduation are full of life change. You can't be sure where you'll want to live, where you'll get a job, how much money you'll make, or if you will get married. Any one of those things could dramatically change which house you buy and how much you have to spend.

The best option for you collegiate, high-achiever types is to rent cheap, stay out of debt (including student loans), and pile up a huge stack of cash. Financially, your big goal should be getting out of school debt-free. Anything over that should go to savings for a while until the dust settles after graduation. If you get a good job quickly and you're ready to settle down in a house, you'll have a fantastic down payment ready to go!

Another time not to buy a house is right after you get married. Those first six to twelve months are full of change and adapting to a new life together. Owning a home and having to deal with all the headaches that come with it add unnecessary stress. Use that time to get to know each other better and to prepare yourselves financially to buy that first house. Buying and owning a home requires solid teamwork if you're married, so focus all your time and effort during those first several months on building a quality relationship instead of a house.

Last, if you know you will be moving in a couple of years, don't buy a home. A home is an investment, and you need to plan on sticking with any investment for at least five years. That way you can ride out any ups and downs in the housing market and turn a profit when you sell the house. If you are going from city to city every couple of years, it's more of a hassle to buy a home and then try and sell it quickly. Your life is already hectic enough with moving so much. Settle the chaos by renting a great home until you're ready to stay in one place for a while.

TERRIBLE MORTGAGE OPTIONS TO AVOID

When you start shopping for a home loan, you are going to hear about a lot of bad mortgage options. We've covered guidelines for what you *should* look for in a mortgage; now let's look at some of the big ones to *avoid*.

Adjustable Rate and Interest-Only Loans

Adjustable rate mortgages (ARMs) are terrible loans that were common in the 2000s. They were also a big reason why we fell into a recession near the end of the decade. Here's how they work: Instead of a fixed interest rate (which means you know exactly how much you're paying in interest over the course of your loan), your rate changes—or adjusts—periodically. That means the rate you agree to at closing could be much lower than what it is a year or two later. These loans leave you at the mercy of volatile interest rates and can drive your monthly payment up every year. Word of advice: just stay away from ARMs.

Interest-only loans were also popular for a while, and they were often paired with ARM loans. With an interest-only loan, you're only paying—you guessed it—the interest. That means you're paying out hundreds or thousands of dollars every month, but you're not actually *buying* anything. If all you do is make the monthly payment, you never gain a nickel of equity in your own home. In fact, it's not much different from renting, but you're still assuming all the risks and expenses of home ownership. Plus, you have to deal with trying to sell it before you can move. You're better off renting than taking on one of these loans.

80/20 Loans

When I told the story of my friend who bought a house with an interest-only ARM loan, I said he had an 80/20 loan. This is when you actually take out two different loans—one for 80 percent and another one for 20 percent, which basically acts as a down payment to help you avoid having to pay PMI. This is 100 percent financing, which means the buyer puts nothing down at all on the house.

At its heart, the 80/20 loan is a creative way for someone to buy a house they can't afford. How do we know they can't afford it? Because they have to borrow their entire down payment!

Balloon Mortgages

The last big offender I want to mention is the balloon mortgage. With a balloon mortgage, you get a loan that looks inexpensive and doesn't require much money up front. However, the "balloon" refers to a balloon payment that is due at the end of a specific term. So, you might be making low monthly payments for five to seven years, but then the balloon comes due and you have to write a huge check all at once. Surprise! Think of these as time-bomb loans, because you never know what will be going on in your life when the balloon comes due. That's too much of a gamble for anyone to take.

The Hidden Costs

My grandfather used to say, "The *cheapest* and *easiest* day of home ownership is the day you close on your house." That's definitely not how it feels when you are sitting at the closing table, seeing all the numbers written out in black print and signing your name a hundred times, but it's true.

My grandfather knew that buying a house meant more than just making the mortgage payments. When you are buying a home, you have to keep in mind that you will need to furnish it as well. And then there's heating and cooling units. Replacing an HVAC can be as much as replacing a car! Then there are the expected but essential costs such as paying the water and electric bill every month. There will be needed repairs around the house from the roof to the foundation and everything in between. And that's just on the inside. Don't forget about keeping up the yard and your property in general. *Buying* a home is costly, but *owning* a home can be even more expensive.

LOVE YOUR HOUSE

There are so many positives of home ownership. You get to build lasting memories in your own space, design and decorate everything perfectly to your tastes, and, in most cases, watch as your property value—and therefore your net worth—increases over time.

You *can* love the life you live and live in a house you love without wrecking your financial future. Buying a home isn't complicated, but it does take time, patience, and discipline. Making the right decision may take starting some new habits, and it may mean breaking some bad ones. I just want you to make the most of the dollars you have by staying out of debt, making wise choices, and ensuring that your home is a blessing instead of a curse.

— Habit 6 —

Think Before You Spend

12

Spending on Purpose

There are some stores you don't appreciate until you are an adult. One of those stores for me is Williams-Sonoma. Once I got married and had a home, this store became a relevant and *exciting* destination.

I was once in a Williams-Sonoma store shopping for a gift for a friend when I saw a set of pots and pans that I wanted in my kitchen. The quality was excellent, and I made a snap decision to buy them. While I stood there, I envisioned using my new set of pots and pans and feeling great about my decision to splurge on some new kitchen necessities.

Reality hit me hard when I looked at the price. The little movie running in my head—using my new pots and pans in our kitchen—came to a screeching halt. Just because I had the cash to spend didn't mean this purchase was a wise decision. Even though this set of cookware could be a great decision *someday*, I realized it wasn't a great decision *that day*. I did one of the hardest things in the world for me, a spender: I walked away from the purchase.

Having the discipline to say no to yourself, even when you have the cash in your pocket, is one of the hardest things about handling money. You see, choosing something good over something bad is easy; anybody can do that. The hard part is when you have to choose between a good thing (great pots and pans) and a better thing (putting that money toward something else). That's when you have to keep your guard up and push through to the wisest decision.

ACTING RICH

Spending money is a subject that's near and dear to my heart. There is absolutely nothing wrong with spending money when you have the money to spend. Going on vacation, upgrading your house, eating out, and shopping are all ways you can use money to enjoy your life and create memorable experiences.

But there is a counterbalance to our spending. How we choose to spend our money affects our present—and our future. The truth is, for a growing number of people, there is a gap between their lifestyle choices and the actual cash they have on hand. Best-selling author Thomas J. Stanley captured this gap perfectly in the title of his book *Stop Acting Rich*. Acting like we're wealthy when we're not only leads us into debt and takes us further away from where we want to be. With every spending and saving decision, we're moving ourselves closer to financial *success* or financial *distress*.

Financing Happiness

Lifestyle choices are a big reason so many people struggle with money. Far too many people want to live a life they can't afford. They drive cars they can't pay for, wear clothes they charged on a credit card, and eat out more often than they should. They chase after a dream of happiness that they see on TV, in their coworkers' lives, or on their long-lost college roommate's Facebook feed. And, when they don't have the actual cash on hand for the things they want, they rack up a pile of debt trying to finance their way to happiness. The problem is, none of these things ever leads to the joy and fulfillment we expect.

Too many people confuse fun with happiness. You can buy fun, like a great vacation or a night out on the town with friends, but you can't buy happiness. Happy is the feeling of hanging out with your spouse, a special weekend getaway with your best friend, or the first time your child grabs onto your finger with her tiny hand. Those are the moments that move us forward, the ones we remember forever—and none of them are for sale.

Needs vs. Wants

When it comes to spending money, there is a difference between *needs* and *wants*. Food, shelter, utilities, clothes, and transportation are *needs*. You need food to survive, a safe place to live, clean clothes to wear, and the means to get to and from work. Those are considered your basic needs. If you have these things, even when times are tough, you'll live on to fight another day.

Online streaming services, cable, fantasy football leagues, and a Halloween costume for your dog are all *wants*. You'd be surprised just how blurred the lines get between needs and wants, even if you stick to just the necessities listed above. There can be a lot of wants hidden in those needs.

For instance, you need a car, but do you need a brand-new car with heated leather seats and a premium sound system? No, that is a want. You need food, but do you need to eat steak dinners every night? No, that is a want. A delicious want, but still a want.

When I am talking about needs, I mean the bare bones of those needs. Put all your purchases through this test. This will help you prioritize your buying decisions. Again, there is nothing at all wrong with buying some wants—as long as they are a reasonable part of your overall plan. I don't want you to walk ten miles to work every day and eat ramen for dinner every night. I just want you to make sure you're taking care of your real needs before you start getting too fancy with your purchases. And, when money is particularly tight— especially now that you're not using debt anymore (right?)—it's helpful to really think through and identify your basic needs. That way, you know exactly what your money priorities are each month.

GROCERY SHOPPING

"How do I shop for groceries and eat healthy on a budget?" Grocery shopping can be a black hole in our budgets because buying food is a part of everyone's life. This is especially true if you prefer healthier food, local meat and produce, or organics. Let's start with the basics of grocery shopping.

Make a List!
A shopping list will always help you stay on track. I use the notes app on my phone and make a list before I go to the store. Not only does it help me avoid impulse purchases, but I also love deleting items off the list once I have them in my cart. It's so gratifying!

Making a list also helps you manage the expectations of kids. When children start to have opinions about the foods they want, we all know the grocery bill has the potential of going up $50—and that's just for after-school snacks. Many kids will do all they can to pressure you into buying things you (and they) don't need. Setting the expectation up front with your child that you're not going to buy anything that's not on the list will help eliminate some of the tantrums on aisle five, but only if you live up to your end of the bargain!

That means *you* don't get anything that's not on the list either. That's easier said than done, I know!

Think of your grocery list as an extension of your budget. You're the boss, so you can make whatever choice you want about what you're going to buy at the store; you just have to decide before you leave home. This will help you stay accountable to the list and your budget.

Meal Planning

I'm a huge fan of meal planning, and if your life is busy, this is a must! This includes planning out your meals for the week, which will also help you figure out what you need to buy.

Meal planning is like budgeting for your food. Knowing the groceries you need to buy a week at a time changes how and where you shop. This also helps reduce impulse buying and junk food purchases. Plus, taking this approach lends itself to batch cooking to help you save time during the week.

If you are making something that will give you two meals' worth of dinners, meal planning helps you figure that out. If I know we're going to make a big pot of white bean chicken chili, I know I will have leftovers I can eat for lunch or even another dinner. And when you plan out what you're going to make in advance, you have the chance to save a little more by looking for the best deals on all the ingredients.

Buy Smart

Smart shopping isn't only about *what* you buy; it's also about *where* you buy. We all know certain stores are more expensive than others, so be mindful of that. Maybe one store has better quality meat while another's produce is perfectly fine and reasonably priced. You can save a lot of money just by shopping around for different products at different stores.

Shop at the store that suits your budget and priorities. If buying organic, shopping in wider aisles, or driving a shorter distance is worth paying a little extra and you have that money budgeted, do it! Simply prioritize what's important and what you can afford. For example, I live in Nashville, where there are two main grocery store chains that compete pretty seriously. One prides itself on lower prices while the other promotes a nicer, more upscale shopping experience. I personally value the *experience* of shopping and going to the store that's closer to my house, so it's worth a few extra dollars to me to shop in the nicer store with the friendlier staff. I'm certainly not against shopping at the more cost-conscious store, but the more upscale store is my go-to grocery place, even though it costs a little extra.

You also want to consider how much your time is worth. Ask yourself, *Am I saving enough money to justify running around to four different stores for the best deals every week?* Some people who do this end up spending more on gas than they save on food. Even if you do save money in the long run, sometimes the savings are so insignificant that the convenience and time savings are worth the few extra bucks you'd spend at one store versus another. Again, think about what you value and plan around that. If shopping at the nicer, more convenient store is your preference and you don't want to drive around looking for the best deal on each item, then just accept the fact that you may have to buy a little less in order to make that work.

Organic

There are many reasonable but differing opinions out there when it comes to buying organic. It can be pretty entertaining to listen to people on opposing sides of the argument: one person needs to know what kind of grass the goat ate before she will eat her goat cheese and the other person eats frozen pizzas for dinner every night.

If you're interested in buying organic food, you might ask yourself if your organic interests are all-or-nothing or if it makes more sense for you to choose organic for only *some* foods. You should spend time researching the cost and true benefits of organic produce, dairy, eggs, meat, and even snacks. Then plan around the organic items that are important to you, but don't be scared to buy the non-organic versions of other food items.

For example, we have a great organic grocery store in my area, but I only drop in there once or twice a month (or less) to pick up a couple of things that I particularly like. I prefer to do my shopping at my regular grocery store. Sure, I have some organic-minded friends who are shocked by this, but I refuse to give into the social pressure to buy organic exclusively. I'm not going to pay $5 for a roll of paper towels, no matter how biodegradable they are.

If you value organics and have an all-or-nothing approach to it, then your food budget is going to be higher. At least admit to yourself that you're prioritizing organic groceries above other things on your budget. You won't magically have more money just because you are focused on superclean eating. So if you want to spend more on food, then you'll have to take that money out of some other areas like clothes or entertainment. If that's what you value, go for it. Just don't assume you can pay for *everything* you value all at once.

Coupons

When it comes to saving money at the grocery store, it would be silly to not include coupons. It's basically free money! Factor in how much time you're spending versus how much you're saving, though. Some people can spend five or more hours a week pouring through coupon websites to save $5 on their weekly grocery bill. Depending on where you are in your financial situation, that may not be the best use of your time.

If you are working on getting out of debt or saving for the emergency fund, coupons should be your best friends. Every dollar you save at the grocery store gets you one dollar closer to being debt-free! But if you are out of debt and are funding retirement, saving $0.75 on juice boxes probably won't make or break your budget.

Growing up, couponing was a part of every Sunday afternoon in our house. My mom was a pro at finding and cutting out coupons from the newspaper. At that time in our lives, it was wise for Mom to take time out of the day, find deals, and take advantage of ways to save money. It would have been unwise for her just to go buy whatever she felt like, no matter the price.

One warning about coupons: they only save you money if you were going to buy the product in the first place. Coupons are a form of marketing. Companies put coupons in newspaper inserts or in the mail because they want you to buy their stuff. So if you buy something you don't need just because you have a coupon for it, you're wasting money—no matter how much you "save."

Buying in Bulk

Another way to spend wisely at the grocery store is to buy in bulk, such as at a warehouse club. Walking into an enormous warehouse full of pallets stacked floor to ceiling of things I could buy does my heart good. I love this kind of store. A warehouse club is a little slice of heaven to a natural spender.

The key with buying in bulk, much like couponing, is to only buy things you know you need and will use. It's easy for me to get carried away in those stores, so I have to be on guard. Winston and I will never use five gallons of honey mustard, no matter how good of a deal it is. However, we buy all of our paper goods, meats, batteries, and dog food in bulk. We shop at a standard grocery store once a week for most food, but the warehouse store is still a great place to buy the things we know we need to have on hand all the time.

Of course, factor your bulk purchases into your monthly budget. If you know you're going to take an expensive trip to the warehouse club every other month, your budget needs to reflect that. You'll spend more money on groceries in the months you stock up on toilet paper, toothpaste, and cases of soda. If you don't plan ahead for it, the trip to the warehouse store will wreck your grocery budget for the month. This is another example of why you need to do a new, original budget every month.

Last, make sure you get your money's worth out of your club fee. Don't buy a membership at one of these stores if you're only going to use it twice a year. Make sure the membership fee is worth the investment. If you aren't saving more money per year than the actual membership costs, you're just throwing money away.

EATING OUT

One of my favorite things in the world is going out to eat. It's a huge weakness for me. I am convinced if I didn't live on a budget, this one thing could make me broke. A night out with Winston or friends at a great Nashville restaurant with appetizers, drinks, and a great meal is my definition of a perfect night out. That's probably because we rarely ate out when I was growing up. Money was tight for so long that we had most of our meals at home. I think that makes me really appreciate being able to go out to eat now.

Priorities

The decision to go out to eat all comes back to priorities. Are you being realistic about your ability to eat out? Is it important enough to you to sacrifice other areas of your budget?

That's how it works: *saying yes to one thing means saying no to another.* Nobody can do it all. If going out to eat regularly is a priority for you, then you must accept the trade-offs of this decision. At the very least, eating out regularly should bring down your grocery bill. If you're spending a ton at the grocery store *and* going out every night, something's off.

If you are on a tight budget but you really want to eat out occasionally, there are easy ways to save money at restaurants. You can eat at a nice place and still order reasonably priced items. Some restaurant portions are often bigger than normal, so consider splitting an entrée and getting an additional side salad. You could also cut out the appetizers and dessert. And, of course, an obvious way to keep some cash in your wallet is to opt for water. You may think this sounds cheap, but if you need to save money, these are great, responsible tips to use when you go out to eat.

Eating out can be hard to say no to, especially if all of your friends go out all the time. You will see pictures on social media of all their great meals, and you'll probably get invited to join them from time to time. But remember that you have to do what's best for your life, not theirs. If there is a season that you have to cut back in this area, do it! Sure, it's a sacrifice, but it'll bring you one step closer to your goals.

Convenience

With busy schedules and hectic lives, sometimes it's easier to pick up dinner on the way home from work or go out to eat on a whim. However, these impulsive meal choices end up costing you more money.

The cost of convenience may be more than you want to pay. If you are a family of four and you choose to eat out at a reasonable restaurant, you'll be lucky to get out of the restaurant—*any* restaurant—for under $50. Do that twice a week for a month and you'll spend $400. If you make the average annual household income of $50,000, that means you're spending a full 10 percent of your income on restaurants!

This is why it's crucial to plan your meals—both at home and at restaurants—each week. There is no perfect science to this. You need to be mindful so you don't get caught in an expensive, although convenient, dinner trap. Adding expenses to your family's plate that you didn't plan for can bust the budget in a hurry.

HOME DÉCOR

Decorating our homes and buying furniture can quickly bust a budget too. At times it was hard for me to accept the fact that I could only decorate one room at a time when Winston and I moved into our first home. I had so many visions for what "home" could and should look like that it would have been easy to get carried away at the furniture and home stores.

You Probably Don't Need a Decorator

Here is some home decorating advice I've picked up. First, you don't need a decorator. Now, if you can afford one and that's what you choose to spend your money on, then do it! But, again, saying yes to a professional decorator will mean saying no to something else. This decision could cost you a lot of money, so be sure you know what you're getting versus what you're giving up.

Don't rush when making decisions on things for your house, even small, everyday additions. You can use great resources like Pinterest, magazines, and even friends. Take your time and make a plan. Don't buy bits and pieces on impulse that you won't like when they're all put together. Then, with your plan in place, make and stick to a budget. Paying cash for your décor and furnishings will force you to move slowly and carefully. The cash habit also makes you a better, wiser consumer.

Again, homes are an easy place for comparisons to sneak in. You have to remember that the way your house is decorated isn't going to change your life. Of course, you want to love your home, but don't let comparing what you have with what someone else has steal your joy in the present.

Repairs, Updates, and Upgrades

Winston and I have a list of anticipated home expenses. This includes everything from updating our living room décor to washing the windows and repainting the trim outside. We have a running list of things we need to do with an estimated total cost next to each item. Then we work our way down that list. As the money comes in, we knock something off the list.

When we were redoing our living room, we had a budget for what we wanted to spend. I often underestimate how expensive these things can be. Something as basic as nice curtains and blinds seem to cost what a semester of college tuition used to. Having that budget in place not only ensures that we're spending only what we can afford, but it also forces us to make better decisions.

If I had the "Let's get everything we want!" mentality when we were redecorating our living room, we wouldn't have put a dime into our retirement accounts for more than a year. At one point, I remember feeling like I wanted to buy everything I saw. But the budget (and a little common sense) didn't let me do that, so I had some choices to make.

If you are a creative person and enjoy making things, there are endless options on how to decorate a home. If this is you, I am jealous! I seriously don't have a creative bone in my body, but I have so many friends who have such a creative eye and can refinish furniture they found at a garage sale or make accessories to hang on their walls. One of my best friends actually came in and helped me style my house. We went to TJ Maxx, I told her my budget, and she helped me pick out things that would work for my home. If you have friends like that, ask them for help. Getting a creative friend's help can get you further, cheaper, than you could get on your own. Just be sure to pay them *something* for their help, even if it's just buying them lunch!

YOUR DECISIONS DETERMINE YOUR DESTINATION

We make a number of decisions every day that will affect our budgets and, ultimately, our futures. It's crucial that you take the time to think before you spend your money. It's not enough to have a budget every month. That's good defense, but you need a strong offense *and* defense to win at most games. The same is true for money.

Know how you'll use your money and when and where you should spend it. Having a budget—a true *spending plan*—will help with this. This habit will also help you discern the difference between needs and wants, because you'll have to make daily decisions about what will and won't get your hard-earned money. A budget doesn't tell you what you *can't* do; it shows you what you *can* do. Making a plan for your money only increases your options.

Buying groceries, eating out, and maintaining a home aren't the only areas where we need a spending plan. These are the everyday choices we make. We also need a spending plan for things like clothes, holidays, and vacations. Can you say *cha-ching*? We can easily overspend on those things, can't we? Let's take a closer look at these areas of spending so we can plan, save, and enjoy!

13

Don't Spend Yourself Broke

One day I came home from a long day of shopping with a smile on my face and some bags in my hands. This hadn't been just any shopping day; this was a shopping day when all the stores at the mall were having sales! I'd saved $70 that particular visit to the mall. $70! Think of all the extra desserts and appetizers I would be able to buy with all that money.

Winston and I crossed paths as I walked through the house to the bedroom to unpack my shopping bags. He knew I had been shopping and was curious about what I had bought.

The first words out of my mouth were, "Babe, you won't believe this! I saved $70 today at the mall." Winston smiled and said, "That's great. How much did you spend?"

"$150," I said. "But listen, I saved $70!"

He laughed. "Yep. That's about right. When you say that, I don't hear that you saved $70. All I hear is that you spent $150." He knows me so well. If I'm not careful, I can fall into the trap of spending money just to save money.

I'm a task-oriented shopper. I rarely go somewhere to browse. I know what I need and where to find it, and then I go get it. If I need a new pair of black shoes or an extension cord for our house, I will accomplish that mission.

What gets me in trouble so often are sales. You would think sales were a good thing, and they can be, but there's something about a SALE! sign that gets my heart pumping. And that's true for a lot of us, isn't it? It's so easy to get distracted by what we can *save* that we lose track of what we can *spend*. In the interest of saving money, we spend money that we never planned on spending. So just be aware when you see those bright, big sale signs in store windows. Sales are a good thing, but only when you were planning to buy the item in the first place.

SHOPPING UNTIL YOU'RE BROKE

When it comes to shopping, you can quickly "save" your way to broke if you're not careful. Much of our unhealthy spending happens when we "$25" ourselves to death without thinking. We make a quick turn into the coffee house drive-through, randomly get a car wash, or make last-minute runs to the hobby store for something. It's easy to spend without *awareness*. Choosing to think about a purchase and managing your impulses will prevent any thoughtless drifting from your spending plan.

Buying Online

Online shopping is a wonderful thing. I don't have to leave my house, navigate through traffic, or fight parking and crowds to get what I want or need. But there are ways shopping online can lead me to spend more money than I intended.

One big danger with online shopping is that it totally removes the element of spending actual cash, which we've talked about before. Spending cash is powerful. It causes a flash of emotional pain where we hesitate to hand that money over sometimes—even if it's a wise, planned purchase. Using a credit card softens that emotional pain quite a bit, but shopping online nearly cuts out the pain completely.

You can spend $1,000 or more just by clicking one single, little button on Amazon. They don't ask if you're sure; they just take the money, put the item in a box, and send it to your house. Listen, I love online shopping, but we have to be super careful here. Don't buy on impulse, and make sure all of those purchases are reflected on your monthly budget. Otherwise, Amazon and other easy-buy sites can really bust your budget.

Also, be aware of the flood of email deals that come from your favorite stores. I get about twenty emails a day from different retailers showing me what their latest products are and what's on sale. When we voluntarily put our addresses on a store's email list, we are asking these companies to flood our inboxes with advertisements. We knowingly invite the daily temptation to buy stuff into our lives. Will Rogers once said, "Advertising is the art of convincing people to spend money they don't have for something they don't need," and that couldn't be more true. So be careful. An email deal is just like a coupon—it's only a good deal if you need the item in the first place.

It's scary how easy buying online is and continues to become. In some cases, it's only a click away. Keep your guard up and discipline yourself to stay on track.

Social Media and App Traps

Retailers know how much time we spend on social media, and search engines know our general interests based on what we have searched for online. Put that together and you get ads targeted directly at you, for something they think you might be interested in, right in the middle of your Facebook and Twitter feeds. You can click a link on your news feed and two minutes later you've bought something. It's easy to be impulsive with the ads that now show up while we're scrolling through our social media feeds.

Even the apps on our phones can unexpectedly cost us money. Smartphone and tablet apps that allow you to buy things like upgrades or lives on a game can cost you more than you realize with a small, one-time or recurring fee. You can start using the apps for free, but it won't be long before you encounter an add-on or upgrade feature that may cost as little as $0.99. Over time, however, those add up, and you may not even be aware that you're doing it. You may find that those extra lives you've been buying for your favorite game aren't actually worth the $20 a month you're spending.

THE PARENT TRAP

When a family is trying to get out of debt and take control of their money, the ones least excited about the changes are the children. Mom and Dad start tightening up the budget and begin paying off their debt in full force. They put some money in savings and start becoming wise shoppers. Of course, when they start saying no to themselves, they will start saying no to their kids too. If those children have been used to getting whatever they want, they aren't going to be enthusiastic about this part of the plan.

When it comes to money and kids, more is caught than taught. The best way to teach your kids how to be wise with money is to be wise with money yourself. With every decision you make for yourself, you're teaching your children how *they* should handle money. The fact is, you can't expect them to win with money later if you aren't doing what it takes to win with money today.

Who Is the Gatekeeper?

Rule number one when it comes to spending on your children is this: kids don't get to choose what you spend your money on. I've talked to far too many parents who tell me the long list of things they *have* to buy for their kids. No. You *have* to clothe, feed, house, and protect your kids. You *don't* have to buy the latest video games, a designer purse, and cell phones. Many parents understand the difference between wants and needs when it comes to their own purchases, but then they throw the principle out the window when it comes to their children. Your kids have needs and wants just like you do, and a wise spender—and parent—knows the difference.

Expect your kids to whine. It's what they do sometimes! If they figure out that a little whining will turn your no into a yes, they'll push that button every time they want something. If you say no to something they want you to buy, be prepared to stick to it. You aren't simply teaching them about money here. You're teaching them about boundaries too. They need to know where you draw the line and that they aren't allowed to cross it.

Part of your job as a parent is to teach them that money is *finite*. If you say yes to everything they want, you're setting an unrealistic expectation for them that they'll always be able to have whatever they want. When they're grown and gone, they'll carry that mentality into adulthood. And when their incomes are unable to provide the things they need, they'll turn to the quick and easy solution: debt. By teaching them limits today, you're protecting them from foolish decisions and piles of debt tomorrow. Don't be afraid to say no! Drawing boundary lines that are determined by your budget is one of the best ways to help your children grow into high-functioning, fully capable adults.

Buying for Your Kids or for You?

Since I was born the year my parents declared bankruptcy, I didn't have a lot of new, fancy things as a little girl. I wore hand-me-down clothes from my sister, and the only "shopping trips" we took were to consignment shops and secondhand stores. We didn't eat in restaurants often, and our vacations consisted of camping trips and afternoons at a little amusement park near our home.

My family's financial situation is different today. When I look at my daughter, all I want to do is buy her the cutest stuff that's out there. It's not because she needs or even wants these things—it's because I want her to have them. There's a big difference. This feeling is a trap, and it can lead you down a dark road of overspending on and spoiling your kids.

There is a difference between wanting your kids to have a better life than you did and trying to live vicariously through them. If you have the budgeted money and you want to take your kids on a great trip or buy them something spectacular, do it. But if you find yourself feeling some internal pressure to buy them things that you always wanted when you were a child, then something is off. You may be buying that item for yourself, not for your child.

In addition, as parents, we can feel the pressure to live up to— or outdo—what other parents are doing for their kids. All that we discussed in the beginning of this book about quitting the comparisons is going to be true here as well. Your family doesn't have to look like and act like everyone else. Doing what's best for your family in the present is what is going to be best for them in the future.

Holidays and Birthdays

Another time you are going to be tempted to spend tons of money is around holidays and birthdays. One way to do that is to budget for Christmas every month, just like you'd budget for a big, once-a-year insurance premium. You know the yearly expense is coming and how much you'll need to spend, so divide it by twelve and add it to your monthly budget. If you usually spend $600 on all your Christmas gifts, for example, just save $50 a month year-round.

Then when the holidays roll around, you aren't in a panic. Instead, you have that cash set aside just for gifts.

Your kids are going to survive if they don't get everything they want. Kids are resilient. They may have a wish list a mile long, but five years later, they won't remember what they got for Christmas when they were nine. But they will remember piling in the car under some blankets as the family drove around looking at Christmas lights. Memories aren't usually made from a heap of plastic junk your kids find under a Christmas tree—they're made out of the time and attention you pour into your children.

Staying away from debt during Christmas is key. Don't let the February You hate the December You. The holidays don't give you a pass on good money management. Stick to that budget to ensure that you truly do have a happy new year!

For many families, birthdays can be an even bigger problem area than Christmas. Remember who you're doing it for. Your one-year-old doesn't care if you have a perfectly themed, over-the-top party complete with food trucks. He wants a fresh diaper and a fistful of birthday cake. The party mentality tends to escalate every year, with parents always trying to outdo what they did the previous year—or worse, trying to outdo what *other parents* did for their kids. I'm convinced that most of the time these elaborate parties are more for the parents than the kids. In the world of comparison living, this can be a sticky trap. Your child's birthday should be a celebration of his or her life. Don't turn it into an opportunity to one-up your friends.

VACATIONS

Vacationing is an area where you can spend wisely if you take the time and plan well.

The most important habit you can get into when it comes to

vacations is to only take trips you can afford. Your income will first go to your needs, then what you have left can go toward things you want—like a great vacation.

Know What You Need

One of the main reasons people feel compelled to take big vacations is to get away from work for a while. If your main driver is simply to take a break, I want to encourage you not to get too carried away with vacation planning.

I've seen some friends approach their vacation planning like it was their full-time job. If you need a break from work, why would you want to turn your vacation into an even more stressful, deadline-driven job? You could return home more tired, broke, and stressed than you were before you left. And I've never heard anyone say, "The kids and I just got back from ten days at Disney, and I feel so relaxed and rested!" Know your vacation motives and plan accordingly.

If you really just need to relax for a few days, a long weekend getaway in a nice, quiet cabin may do the trick for a lot less money. But if you do want the full, crazy, active, week-long destination vacation with the whole family, then go for it! Just be warned: This isn't the kind of trip you'll be able to do on impulse. Trips to see Mickey usually take months—or even years—of planning. And you know what that means . . .

Budget, Budget, Budget

From this day on, taking a big, expensive vacation on a whim is probably not going to happen. I'm sorry. I wish I could say otherwise, but I can't. If the only way you can spontaneously go to Hawaii is by either wiping out your emergency fund or putting the whole thing on a credit card, that's probably not a great plan. Both of those are terrible ideas that can crush you financially.

If you want to take a $6,000 trip twelve months from now,

then it's time to get to work. You need a "Vacation" line on your budget, and that line needs to get $500 of your money every month between now and then. That means you can't buy $2,000 worth of plane tickets for at least four months, so this can impact *when* you take your trip if you have to book everything in advance.

When I explain this to some people, I can see their hearts sink right in front of me. The dream of an exotic family trip can be so enticing, but when they see the $500 monthly price tag the dream requires, they realize it honestly doesn't make sense in their financial situation—for now, at least. I hate that for them, but what I'd hate even more is for them to take the trip anyway and bring home a mountain of credit card debt that would take years to pay off. Don't ruin such a special trip by setting yourself up to hate the memory of it three years from now. Save like you mean it, remember? That includes vacations. Until you have the cash available, consider taking a big trip every few years with smaller trips in between.

Once you're on the trip—whether it's a big, once-in-a-lifetime excursion or just a weekend trip to the beach—the worst thing you can do is say, "We're on vacation! Let's just spend money and enjoy. We'll worry about the cost later." I have been known to say this a time or two. The hard reality is that all those debit-card charges still count even when you're out of town. You might enjoy it for the moment, but a week later, reality will come crashing in on you. Don't put a dark cloud of regret over a vacation with your family. You want your smile to be just as big *after* the trip as it is in all the vacation pictures. Remember, the money you saved for the trip should be guilt-free spending, so enjoy it!

I know this is a drum I can't stop beating, but when it comes to vacations, remember not to compare your trip—or your lack of trips—to everyone around you. Don't let the photo of a friend's feet in the sand with the ocean in the background steal the joy of your long weekend getaway to a cabin in the woods. And don't let your neighbors' vacation pictures be the motivator for your trip. This is an easy place to compare because our social media feeds are full of vacation photos.

Charge It to "Cash," Not the Room

One thing that's even easier than swiping a card is saying that dangerous little phrase, "Oh, just charge it to the room." Those magic words remove every bit of friction from making a purchase. You can spend money without even thinking about it. It's the verbal equivalent of Amazon's 1-Click purchasing button.

Most hotels and resorts make it easy for you to spend money on their property. If your local grocery store tried to charge hotel and resort prices for food and drinks, you'd laugh and move along. But if a resort offers the service of delivering these items to your room, you'd not only pay the crazy prices, but you'd tip and thank whoever brings those things to you!

Cut Your Costs

If you're looking for one big way to cut costs on a family vacation, here it is: make your own meals. "But Rachel! Eating out is part of what makes a vacation so special!" I know! If you've got plenty of budgeted money to spend, and eating out is a priority for you, go for it! However, if the destination is a higher priority than the meals, try eating most of your meals in the room.

Vacation planners tell you to plan on $50 to $100 a day per person on food. Taking a trip to the grocery store instead of the steak house once you get to your destination can save you hundreds on the trip.

Winston's family has a tradition of going to the beach each year around spring break. His parents rent a big house, and we all get together for a week. We eat most of our meals in the home, and each couple prepares one dinner during the week. We eat in four nights, and then we go out the other two nights. That routine works really well for us, especially since there are little kids running around. Sometimes it's more relaxing for parents if the kids can run wild at a home or hotel instead of at a restaurant.

Extended Family Vacations

Now that many of my friends are married with little kids, I'm starting to notice a trend when it comes to vacations. We're seeing these huge family trips where an older couple invites their adult kids and grandkids on a big family getaway. My own family does this, and I love getting away with my parents, my sister's family, and my brother. We love spending time together, and we all love to travel. These vacations mean the world to me.

These trips can also be tricky, though, when it's unclear who is paying for what. In some families the grandparents will pay the whole bill for everyone to go. In others, the grandparents make the plans but expect their adult children to pay their own way. Either way is fine, as long as everyone is on board with the decision.

Too often, though, someone in the family makes crazy plans and simply expects everyone else to fall in line. The problem is, everyone may be at different places financially. A $1,000 getaway next month may not be a big deal for you, but it could be devastating to your brother's family. When planning big family trips, everyone has to be up front and honest about what they can do, and everyone else needs to respect those decisions.

If your parents want to take your family on a great trip and pay for everything, take off and have fun! But if they expect you to pay your own way on a trip you didn't plan (or maybe even don't want to go on), it's time for a talk with Mom and Dad. You remember we said that your kids don't get to decide how you spend your money, right? Well, the same is true for your parents. If you don't have the money to take the trip, or if you have other priorities for your money, then the answer should be a graceful no. There's no shame or guilt in that! Do what's best for your own family—even if it means disappointing your parents.

If you do decide to go, set reasonable expectations on the front end and be sure that everyone's on the same page. Eliminate surprises where you can. Are you expected to pay for your amusement park tickets, airfare, hotel room, or part of the house that was rented? Are you expected to pay for your own meals? If so, how many? All of them? Are you expected to pay for your own travel?

Nothing ruins a family trip like getting to a restaurant and not knowing who is going to pick up the tab. If you're at the end of the vacation and it's time to pay the bill, not having had this conversation in advance will create an awkward situation. If no one steps up to pay, you may feel like you need to cover the bill because talking about it would be too weird. Now you're paying for something you weren't expecting to, and it can put a dark cloud over the vacation and the relationships with family members.

Talk about all of this stuff beforehand. It's not rude or disrespectful to your parents or siblings to ask for an open and honest conversation. Everyone else is probably hoping *someone* will step up with the courage to raise the subject. Your boldness could save not only you, but also your other family members from a financial and emotional mess.

Where things get tricky is if you're expected to pay for some things, but you don't have the money—or you are choosing to put all your extra money toward paying off debt. As uncomfortable as it might be, you need to share that with whoever is planning or coordinating the trip. The honesty might seem harsh and your parents might not be happy, but you need to do what's best for you. That doesn't mean you are saying no to family trips for the rest of your life—it's just for a short period of time. There will be other trips, but *this one* might not be the best use of your money right now.

Stay Away!

Another vacation trap you want to avoid are some of the deals you encounter. Many of these can be found online. Some of these deals are legit and great. Others are rip-offs and are too good to be true.

I once saw a TV commercial for a travel website that set this up perfectly. A gentleman books a vacation from the website, and the place looks gorgeous. Beautiful pictures of white sands, open beaches, and crystal-clear, blue water beckon him as he books his trip. Then the camera pans to him arriving at the destination—there's trash and broken glass everywhere, barely any place to walk, and he can see a few dorsal fins in the distance. Don't be like that guy! Look around, do your research, and know what you're getting yourself into.

Next, avoid time-shares altogether. They're the easiest contracts to walk into, but some of the hardest to get out of. The only way to get out of a time-share deal is to sell it, but that'll be next to impossible because no one wants it. Don't even go to the presentation. I promise, the free breakfast they give you won't be worth the relentless sales pressure and emotional wringer they'll put you through.

A time-share just gives you an expensive piece of real estate that you can't sell and that you only get to enjoy one or a few weeks out of the year. It also locks you into the same vacation spot year after year for decades because you'll feel pressured to go back every year since you're still paying for it. Keep your options open. If you want to hit the same beach every year, then do it! But at least give yourself the freedom to pick new and exciting places to stay.

Be Cheap—Or Don't

Many cities have great free attractions for families. They can help you save money and add some variety to a trip if needed. Look around and ask locals for suggestions. There are a lot of memory-making, fun things to do for free if you get creative and do your research.

But if you have saved up for this vacation and you have money set aside to spend, then spend it! Enjoy your hard work and patience by allowing yourself to buy something you want. You will find that the more you save up and have to spend on a trip, the more enjoyable it seems. Sometimes it's worth putting the trip off a few months to get some extra cash in the bank so you can enjoy some luxury while relaxing on a fun vacation.

TAKE CONTROL OF YOUR SPENDING

Food, clothing, homes, birthdays, holidays, vacations—all of these things demand spending decisions that reflect what's truly important to us.

However, there is nothing worse than working long, hard hours for your money and then wondering where it all went. That will leave you feeling broke and broken. But even if that's where you've been up to this point, I have good news: Your past doesn't have to dictate your future. You can make decisions and create new habits today that will change the course of your future. There is hope, but it begins with focusing your attention now and taking control of your spending. Remember, think before you spend!

— Habit 7 —

Give a Little . . .
Until You Can Give a Lot

14

A Lifestyle of Giving

One of our best friends is a pretty incredible guy. He has dedicated his life to helping young men in the inner city who don't have a father figure in their lives. Our friend has stepped into this community, and people have fallen in love with him and his heart. He has built relationships with these teenage guys and has helped them walk through some pretty tough situations. He does everything from taking them to school to picking them up from football practice to buying them groceries if food is low in their home. He'll do just about anything for them.

The impact he's made in the lives of these young men and their families is pretty remarkable. He's become exactly what they need most—a stable friend and mentor in the middle of their hectic world. When I think about giving, I think about this guy. And it's not just the giving he's doing with his own life that's inspiring, but it's also the way others in our community have come around him to support him financially. We all feel a connection to him and his incredible ministry, and we want to join together to contribute to the work he is doing.

Generosity isn't a simple act of giving or a grand event. Generosity is a *lifestyle* that changes hearts and minds as it blesses everyone involved. I have learned over the years that giving is the most fun you can have with money. And I have to say, I am hooked.

OUTRAGEOUSLY GENEROUS

The habit of giving is the exclamation mark when it comes to our money. Improving your bank account isn't the primary purpose of good money habits. While that's important, it isn't where your journey with money should end. As you bring your money into alignment with your values, you begin to see how what you have to give—your time, money, and abilities—can become instruments of grace that can impact the trajectory of others' lives forever.

Having good money habits in place will help you find peace of mind. You will get to live life on your terms instead of the bank's. You'll build wealth and buy the things that are important to you. You'll get out of debt once and for all. You'll communicate with your spouse, kids, and others at a deeper level. But as wonderful as those things are, they aren't the end goal. Ultimately, you want to win with money so you can become an outrageous giver!

Giving can be a difficult topic for people to understand because they don't know why or how they should give—but once you've answered those questions for yourself, there will be no turning back.

Why Should I Give?

Something happens to your heart when you give—something that changes you for the better. It's easy, even natural, to live in a selfish state of mind. Our entire culture is based on an attitude that demands "me first" and instant gratification. And our lives are often centered on what makes us happy. *What do I want to do? How do I look? Where should we go?* It's tempting to spend most of our energy each day answering these questions for ourselves.

And if giving isn't already a lifestyle for you, becoming a generous person can seem counterintuitive. It can feel like an uphill battle at first. But as you begin to shift your focus from fulfilling your own needs and wishes to meeting the needs of others, you change. You learn what it means to be truly happy. It really is true that generous people are not only the happiest people on the planet, but they also truly live more fulfilling lives.

Selling the American Dream

One powerful story of generosity is captured in the book *The Power of Half* by Hannah and Kevin Salwen.[1] It's a story about an average American family who worked hard and achieved much. At the beginning of the book, they have everything most people strive their whole lives to obtain. They drive new cars, live in a big house, and have lots of nice stuff.

Then Hannah Salwen, only fourteen years old at the time, becomes restless about the homeless people in her city. Her parents encourage her desire to help, but nothing dramatically changes in the family's lifestyle. Over the course of months and years, her passion to help others moves her parents so much that they decide to sell their home and give half of the proceeds to charity. The sum total of the amount they gave away was about $800,000.

This family's journey taught me that every person has a choice to make with what they've been given. It doesn't matter if you have a lot or a little. Generosity is something everyone can practice. Now, don't freak out. I'm not saying that once you start practicing generosity that you'll end up selling your house and giving away half the money. That was a pretty unique call on one family's life. However—and this is the thing that might *really* surprise you—you might find that you *want* to start doing stuff like that. It may start small, like maybe a $50 tip on a $10 restaurant bill to help a struggling server who's working on Thanksgiving Day. But the impact of even small acts of generosity can have a powerful and far-reaching ripple effect. It changes everyone involved, starting with you.

People who love their money and stuff more than they love other people will live small, lonely, and ultimately ineffective lives. There is room for you to build wealth and enjoy the things money can buy. We've talked about that throughout the book, and it's what I want for you. But the endgame for practicing good money habits is not to buy so much stuff for ourselves that it fills up our garages and rented storage units. The real goal with building wealth is to leave a measurable and meaningful mark on the people around you.

I believe that our culture is struggling with the diseases of selfishness and discontentment, and generosity is the only cure I know.

What the Bible Says About Giving

Another reason I give is because giving is a foundational part of my Christian faith. I understand that you may not share my beliefs, but it's hard to dismiss the wisdom in the Bible's financial teaching. Throughout the Scriptures you can find clear teaching on budgeting, debt, saving, spending, comparison living—everything we've covered in this book so far. And, of course, the Bible also has a lot to say about giving.

Jesus talked more about money in the New Testament than anything else—including heaven and hell. Why is that? Because money is never *just* about money. What you and I do with our money is evidence of what we believe. Whether it's giving to your local church or directly to help others in need, the act of giving is something beautiful. Giving *changes* us—both in the giving and the receiving.

The first thing that changes, I think, is our perspective on ownership. The Bible says, "The earth is the LORD's, and the fulness thereof" (Psalm 24:1 KJV). He owns the whole world and everything in it—including my stuff. If He is the owner, then I am just the manager. He lets me use and enjoy a portion of His wealth, but I never lose sight of the fact that it's not really mine. Giving money away is simply a reminder of my position and my role in the world. Scripture says we were all made in the image of God. If God is the biggest giver of all, then I am, by design, supposed to be a giver too. Generosity is a part of my spiritual DNA.

Two people immediately come to mind for me when I think about the power of giving. They are a married couple who are now in their eighties. He is a retired surgeon. She was a stay-at-home mom. They decided early in their marriage to live on no more than 10 percent of their earnings. Granted, they were living in a multimillion-dollar home and enjoying all the trappings of the well-funded life. But all this came out of only 10 percent of their income.

They made it a personal mission to alter their lifestyle so they could use what God had given them to help others. This couple would never want you to think of them as heroic or inspirational but simply as living from a place of personal faith. We've been talking a lot in this book about setting your finances up in such a way that you can spend money on the things you value. Well, this couple valued giving, and they set their lifestyle around that conviction.

I'm not suggesting that you live on 10 percent of your income (unless God's put that specific call on your heart), but what I hope you take away from this story is that this couple was open to giving whatever they felt called to give. They live with an open hand, and, in doing so, they are an encouragement and blessing to those around them. Throughout their entire adult lives, they made giving a priority and centered their finances on that one thing because it's what they valued.

GIVING AND YOUR FINANCIAL PLAN

Whenever I talk about giving, someone usually comes up to me and says something like, "Rachel, all that sounds amazing. I'd love to be able to give to people in need and to causes I believe in. When do you think I'll have enough money to be able to give generously?"

If that's you, I have good news for you: you can start today! That's right; I believe that giving should always be part of your financial plan, no matter how much *or* how little you have. Even if you think you can't afford it, I encourage you to work some giving into your budget. This is a critical money habit you need to develop if you want to win with money. I believe this habit is just as important as the others we've discussed, including saving, budgeting, and staying out of debt. If you do all of those things but leave giving out of your plan, your life will always be out of balance.

Getting Started

Every day is an opportunity to start becoming a more generous person. You always need to be giving no matter where you are financially. If you're getting out of debt or saving up for that emergency fund, then try giving a little right now. If you are debt-free with a full emergency fund and retirement savings underway, then you can find some bigger opportunities to make a difference.

I teach people to give off the top of what they make. That means giving should be the first line on your budget unless you honestly don't have enough money to cover your basic necessities. If you put giving (or saving, for that matter) at the bottom of the list, you'll never get to it. Something else will always seem more important, so make giving a priority. If you've never given regularly before, I suggest starting with 10 percent of your income each month. If that sounds intimidating, start smaller while you get used to it and then increase it over time.

The amount doesn't even matter when you're just getting started. The point is to start with something and make it a regular part of your lifestyle. The goal is to make this a habit, and that means you've got to find ways to give often. Over time, the habit starts to take hold, and giving will not only feel perfectly natural, but you'll also feel like something important is missing if you go too long without doing it.

Giving Even When It's Tight

You may be in a tight place with your money, but don't let that stop you from experiencing the joy of giving. That said, make sure you can cover your rent or mortgage, your transportation, clothes to wear, and food to eat. Go back to the budget and make sure you are covering your basic needs. I'm not a fan of the "give until it hurts" philosophy; I'm more of a "God loves a cheerful giver" kind of person (2 Corinthians 9:7). It's hard to give cheerfully if doing so means your kids won't have dinner this week. So, while I want you to develop a habit of generous giving, I don't want you to put your family in danger. Make sure your basic needs are covered, and then start giving.

With your basic needs taken care of, you should have some room to give. Making giving a priority, though, may mean making some difficult judgment calls on some of the wants in your life. It may mean some stuff has to go.

If you have to take your two thousand cable channels down to five hundred in order to free up some extra cash to give, the exchange will be worth it. You will get more out of life helping that single mom out with Christmas than with the fifteen hundred cable channels you are missing. Even then, those fifteen hundred channels are not gone for good. Once you get better control of your money and are in a position to get those channels back, then do it!

If you find yourself in a position where you can't afford to give even a small amount of money, then set a date for when you can start giving. Don't throw it too far in the future, however. I'm talking about sometime in the next thirty to sixty days. That should be plenty of time to make some changes and free up some cash to give. If you make a plan for your money with a budget and stick to that budget, you should be able to find a way to start giving regularly in short order. Start where you are, and then you can grow your level of giving over time.

Give Even While Getting Out of Debt

People often ask if they should give even while they're working to pay off their debt. While you want to get out of debt as fast as you can, giving should be part of your plan as you work the debt snowball. All of the habits we've talked about work together to help you win with money overall. Developing these habits is not just about changing your attitude about debt, saving, and spending but changing your whole relationship with money. Giving at every step in the process does that more effectively than anything else.

As you stay focused over time, you'll find that you can give while paying off your student loans, car payments, credit cards, and mortgage. This is exactly what my parents did as they climbed out of the black hole of bankruptcy. My earliest memory of giving took place in church. Every week, I sat in my seat on the pew and watched my parents as the offering bag came by. Even as a young child, I understood that money was tight. I knew my dad was working all day and night to get the family back on our feet. Every dollar mattered, not only to us, but also to the company he had just started to build. Even though the stakes were high, my mom and dad put a folded check in the red velvet offering bag every week, without fail. For them, giving was a non-negotiable.

Flexing Your Giving Muscles

I've learned that what you do when times are hard is a good indicator of what you will do when things are going well. Whatever was written on those checks my parents gave doesn't compare to their capacity to give now. But if they hadn't committed to a habit of giving and generosity then, I doubt they'd be as generous as they are today.

John D. Rockefeller, generally regarded as the wealthiest man in US history, may have said it best: "I never would have been able to tithe the first million dollars I ever made if I had not tithed my first salary, which was $1.50 per week." That was a long time ago, but if you can only afford to give $1.50 a week right now, then start there. Like I said before, the dollar amount isn't the issue. The real issue is the habit you're building—the attitude you're developing about giving in general. That's why I call this habit "Give a little . . . until you can give a lot."

You see, I know that if you will start flexing those giving muscles even when you don't have much to give, you'll not only set yourself up to *be able* to give a lot in the future, but you'll also set yourself up to actually *want* to.

TOWARD A LIFE OF GIVING

A friend recently told me about something her five-year-old daughter had become passionate about. The little girl had learned in Sunday school about a local family who was trying to raise enough money for their child to get an important medical procedure. The teacher encouraged all the kids to collect pennies, nickels, and dimes during the week and bring them to church the next Sunday. Then they would collect all the money from all the classes and send the money to an organization that would help fund the medical procedure.

This little girl wasn't satisfied with the amount of pennies, nickels, and dimes she found around the house. She asked her parents to help, then her grandparents, and then just about anyone she came into contact with that week. On Saturday night my friend sat down with her daughter to count all the money she had collected.

My friend said, "Honey, you did great! I'm so proud of you. I'm sure that little girl will be happy you helped her get the help she needed."

Her daughter responded, "Mommy, that's not enough." She thought for a moment and then left the table. She came back a few minutes later with a handful of crumpled up bills in her hands—another $12 from the jar she was using to save up for a new doll.

My friend teared up at this point. She asked her, "Are you sure you want to give away all the money you've been saving? You don't have to do that."

The little girl said, "Yes. I want to." In total my friend's daughter took more than $100 to church with her on Sunday. At five years old, she had learned that it's not enough to simply ask other people to give; she wanted to participate in the giving herself. A life of giving was the life she wanted.

That's exactly what I want for you—a great start. It doesn't matter where you are, how old you are, or how much you have. It doesn't matter if you have a little to give or a lot to give. What matters is the decision to make giving a key habit in your life. When you do that, you'll unlock the power to totally change your relationship with money. You'll be set up to win and give like you never thought possible, and, I promise, it'll be an amazing journey.

15

How to Give

It was one of those days for the both of us. When Winston and I got home after work, we both just knew the other had a similar day—not anything out of the ordinary or really bad, just a long, exhausting day.

We were too tired to cook, so we decided to go out for dinner. We didn't go to a fancy, expensive place—just a local restaurant we knew we could count on for good food, friendly service, and a relaxing atmosphere.

As we walked into the restaurant we saw an older couple that I had known most of my life. We caught up briefly and then followed the hostess to our table. We ordered our favorite meals and sat talking to each other. It was fun to laugh at stuff that had happened during the day and enjoy some downtime together.

As dinner was ending, we asked the server for the bill. He said, "It's been taken care of. The couple who was seated over there paid for your meal." We were both shocked and grateful at the same time—and just blown away that they would think to do that.

That single act of kindness changed our whole attitude about the day. We went to bed that night smiling and feeling grateful, which was definitely not the attitudes we had when we first got home from work. Someone cared enough to step into our lives, just for a second, and it made an impact that we're still talking about years later.

BACK TO BASICS

Often we think about giving in huge, world-changing terms. We think about making a significant contribution to a missionary or helping an organization dig wells in Africa. Those are great causes—but if that's all we think of, we have a limited view of giving. The small, spur-of-the-moment acts of kindness make a difference too and can completely turn someone's life around. And it's just so much fun to give to others—especially when they're not expecting it.

As we thought more about that simple act of kindness in the restaurant, Winston and I expanded our view of giving. We started looking for little ways we could impact other peoples' lives every day. But generous giving can get complicated. There are lots of ways you can give—from individuals in need to seemingly endless non-profits doing good things to an infinite number of "add-on" gifts that you can make while you're checking out at the grocery store. How do you know when it's the right time to give, who you should give to, and how you can be generous without breaking the bank? Let's talk about it.

Percentage Giving

As a Christian, I believe giving begins with the local church. Winston and I give 10 percent of our income to our church—as a starting point. That percentage is what's written at the top of our budget. We always put giving first to keep money in the proper perspective.

Where you give is totally up to you and your family, making sure that your giving follows your personal values. We follow what Scripture says and give 10 percent—or a tithe—to the local church to support their ministry and mission. When we give above and beyond that 10 percent baseline, we direct that money to other causes that Winston and I believe in.

It's hard to start your giving at 10 percent if you're not used to giving at all. A pastor once challenged his congregation to increase their giving 1 percent over the previous year. His goal was to get everyone to participate in the giving process. He knew that going from zero to 10 percent was going to be too steep a climb for some. By suggesting everyone give just 1 percent more, giving became manageable for everyone in the congregation. He gave them a practical, unintimidating place to start. If you stretch slowly from where you are, you'll be amazed just how generous you can become.

Again, 10 percent shouldn't be the final goal but only the beginning. Consider the surgeon and his wife we talked about in the previous chapter. What if you set a lifetime goal to increase your giving—even by only 1 percent—every year of your working lifetime? You probably wouldn't even notice the "missing" 1 percent year to year, but think about the impact you could have and the legacy you could build.

The cool thing about percentage giving is that it grows right along with your income. As you earn more, you give more. It's automatic. You don't have to think about it. Plus, if you're used to living on 90 percent of your income every month and then you get a raise, you still get to feel the impact of that raise. After the pay increase, you'll give more *and* you'll bring more home every month. It's not like you're giving up your Christmas bonus every year!

Don't let fear or intimidation keep you from building a habit of giving. Start where you are and, like we discussed in the last chapter, begin flexing those giving muscles with whatever feels comfortable right now.

The "Easy" Button

Winston and I set up auto drafts for the gifts we make on a recurring basis, such as our tithe to our church. I travel a lot, and our schedules are crazy at times. Putting our recurring giving on autopilot ensures we are giving regularly even if we're out of town most of the month.

The only problem with this is that I sometimes don't feel like I am giving at all. It can easily become "out of sight, out of mind." Because it is so automated, I don't always feel like I am giving up something or even emotionally connected to the money I'm giving away. That's why it's important for us to give to other things as well. Sometimes it's good to feel the struggle. That mild discomfort is a constant reminder that the money is not mine to begin with—all of it belongs to God, and He's given it to me to manage.

Now let's talk about how people with variable incomes—those who don't make the same set amount every month—should give. If you fall into this category, you might feel like you can't put your giving on autopilot because you don't know how much you'll make in a month. Winston and I both have variable incomes, so we do our best to estimate our income at the beginning of each month. That's what we base our monthly auto withdrawal amount on. Then we check our giving in relation to our income throughout the year and at the end of the year. If we underestimated our income, we simply write a check for the difference.

If you are just starting out, give with cash or a check. There is something powerful about the physical experience of giving money away. Auto drafting your giving is convenient, but it can be easy to forget about since you don't have to take any action to make it happen. As giving becomes more and more of a habit, and as you grow to enjoy the experience of giving, then start exploring automated systems to make things easier.

Tax-Deductible

A side benefit of giving is that any money you give to a legally designated nonprofit or religious organization is tax-deductible. That shouldn't be your *reason* for giving, but if you're giving anyway, you should take advantage of the deduction. This requires some record keeping, though.

You'll need to keep a receipt of the gift. If you give online, a receipt should be automatically generated for you. Print it out or keep a copy for your records. You'll need it in case you are ever audited. If you use a CPA or other tax-preparation service, they'll need it to verify your total charitable contributions for the year. Many organizations will send you an end-of-year giving statement for your taxes, but don't count on it. Keep your own records throughout the year just in case.

Keep in mind that not every organization qualifies for a tax deduction. Be sure to do your homework to avoid any tax-time surprises. One easy way you can tell is if you see the 501(c)3 designation at the bottom of the organization's website or in the printed materials. This is a tax status granted by the federal government that allows the organization the ability to receive tax-deductible gifts.

If you're not sure, you should contact the organization directly or do a little research online. Credible organizations will always be up-front about their tax status. If an organization you are considering giving to is ambiguous about their status or, worse, they outright refuse to discuss it, stay away!

Include Your Children

Create an opportunity to include your children in your giving as a family. They may not understand all the details, but they will remember that you gave to others.

Even if you prefer giving electronically, you may want to write actual checks for a season of life just so your kids can watch you physically give the money away. Again, watching my parents give every week is a powerful memory for me. They didn't make a big show of it. There were no flashing lights, and Dad never yelled, "Hey, kids! Look, I'm giving!" They just set a stable, consistent example of what giving looks like.

Like I've said before, I believe more is caught than taught. Your kids are watching your example, so show them what giving looks like. Make sure they know you are giving, even if you aren't telling them dollar amounts. And if you are giving electronically, find ways to include them in the process.

Anonymous Giving

Sometimes, I think the best kind of giving is when no one knows it was you. We've talked about how money changes relationships, and this is true even in the world of giving. People get awkward and weird about money, and that discomfort too often gets in the way of someone getting the help they need. They may not accept a huge financial gift from "Joe and Suzie," but they will probably be over the moon with gratitude for an anonymous gift that meets a specific need and leaves them scratching their heads.

A friend of mine told me about an experience she and her husband had that changed their lives completely. He had heard about a family at work who had lost everything in a fire, including their only vehicle. While her husband didn't know the people directly, he knew that they didn't make enough to replace everything they had lost. One night over dinner, he told his wife (my friend) about the family and mentioned that he wanted to do something to help them—but without drawing attention to himself.

Then he dropped a bombshell. They had been saving up for a new ski boat so the kids could learn to water ski. He suggested that instead of getting the boat, they use the money to buy a minivan for this family. He reasoned that if they had a safe place to stay, food to eat, clothes to wear, and a dependable vehicle, then they could get back on their feet. My friend was stunned by her husband's suggestion, but she and their kids thought it was a great idea. They all agreed it was the best thing they could do with that money.

That next day he told his boss, the CEO, what he and his family had decided to do for this family. The catch, though, was that he wanted to give the van without anyone ever knowing it was them. His boss took the check and the company purchased the vehicle for the family. The cool part is the CEO allowed my friends to present the vehicle to the family in need on behalf of the company. She talked about how much it meant to their kids—and that it will leave an impression on them for a lifetime.

It doesn't matter whether or not someone knows it was you. Sometimes that's appropriate, and sometimes it's not. Either way, the act of giving changes your relationship with money and with the people around you.

THINK BEFORE YOU GIVE

If you want the money you give to make a difference, then you need to be thoughtful about where and to whom you give. You want your decision to count. That will require a little extra effort on your part in the beginning. But once you've landed on an organization or a person you feel comfortable supporting, you'll have confidence each time you give, knowing that your dollars will make a difference.

Start with the Budget
The first place to start is the charity's budget. It's acceptable and reasonable to want to see a copy of it. All reputable nonprofits will

make this available to you. Some will do so on their website. Others ask that you call in and request a copy. Either way, if an organization is not willing to give you this information, see that as a red flag and look somewhere else.

And don't feel bad about doing this. You should want to know if your money will be used in the way you think is best. If not, it takes the fun and comfort out of giving because you can't trust how it will be used. Don't give blindly. Make sure you are comfortable with how the organization takes in and uses money.

The sad truth is, many nonprofits are terrible at managing their money. People give generously because they think they're helping a worthy organization—but then wasteful, sloppy accounting and business practices eat up almost every penny of every donation. Even if the cause is a good one, if you give to a poorly run nonprofit, your money won't be as effective.

Think of your giving dollars like your investing dollars. You wouldn't make a financial investment without digging into the details, right? The same is true when giving to a charity. Dig in and ask questions. Do some research. Search online for tools and resources to learn how well different charities manage their money. There are a few reputable organizations that actually rate different nonprofits the way the Better Business Bureau would rate a business. Seek out these services and take the time to find out everything you can about the nonprofit before you give a donation.

Will there be times when you feel the urge to give without doing any research? Sure! But overall, be a diligent and wise giver. You are investing in the future of our world, so do it wisely.

Make the Best Decision

There are a lot of options when deciding on your charitable giving—so many choices that it can seem intimidating if you don't know where to start. You might choose your church or a charity. Or maybe you want to give to an individual who needs help. Sometimes it's to your friends or family. This can be true if they are raising money for something like a mission trip, or if they are in a self-supporting ministry position and you choose to become a financial partner.

Whatever the situation or opportunity, remember that you aren't going to personally solve all the world's problems through one gift and one organization. Besides, that's not your job. You can't always say yes. What you do with your money is completely your decision. No one else should make your spending decisions for you, and the same is true for your giving decisions. Just because someone asks doesn't mean you have to say yes—even when it's family.

Just a reminder: If a friend or family member needs some financial help, make sure you *give* that money to them free and clear. Do not loan money to people—especially friends and family. If they need help and you have the money and the inclination to help, that's great. But give it away with no strings attached.

Deep and Wide

When it comes to your giving, consider the "deep and wide" approach. You can make a big impact on a few things or a small impact on many things. For example, there is the "nickel and dime" approach to giving where you give whenever the checkout cashier asks for money for a charity (usually by adding a dollar to the total or donating the coins you'd get back). While adding a dollar to your grocery bill might be a good idea every now and then, think of ways you can make a bigger impact than just a dollar here and there. It's not bad to give in those instances, but think about the deep and wide mind-set. What do you want to do? Whatever you decide, be intentional with that choice and follow through.

You will make the most impact when you partner with an organization through a recurring gift and build a relationship with them over time. This is something you'll never get by giving a dollar here and a dollar there. You're also more likely to see, or even participate, in the direct delivery of the work you are supporting. You can't go deep with every cause or charity, but pick one or two. That will shorten the distance between your dollar and the difference you can make.

Winston and I are careful about how we use our charitable dollars. We take it seriously. Unless I feel a huge tug on my heart, I politely decline when the cashier asks for a donation. I used to have a paragraph-long explanation on why I was not giving a dollar. But now I'm okay saying no at times because we have researched, asked budgeting questions, and invested a great deal of time, emotion, and money into the places and people we support. This may sound clinical, but it keeps me on track. If I feel led to give to something spontaneously, I will listen to that nudge—but more often than not, I don't randomly give.

MORE THAN JUST MONEY

What else can you offer when you are giving? Is it just your money? No. You can give much more than just that. Former First Lady Barbara Bush once said, "Some people give time, some money, some their skills and connections, some literally give their life's blood. But everyone has something to give." With this in mind, I suggest you divide your giving into three categories: time, abilities, and money. Giving doesn't always have to result in an exchange of dollars. You have ways to give over and above the money you give to others.

Volunteer Your Time and Attention

In addition to your money, be generous with your most valuable asset, namely time spent investing in other people's lives. One of my first mentors was like this. She was the most generous person I had ever met—not just with her money, but also her time and attention. She was always willing to talk, spend time with me, and answer my questions. She was genuinely interested in my life. She lived her life through the lens of serving and helping others. And as a recipient of that love, I wanted to be like her.

This early mentor made such a huge impact on me that, when I was in college, I volunteered with a ministry that paired college-aged mentors with high school students in local schools. I spent a lot of time with a great group of girls, and I walked with them for three years. Helping them navigate the challenges of high school was a blast. Looking back, I got more out of that time than those high school girls did.

When you give—especially when you give your time— it changes you. Generosity shapes you into a more selfless person. And selfless people simply live more joyful, fulfilled, and satisfied lives. When you experience generosity yourself, like I did with my first mentor, you find yourself wanting to pass that blessing along to someone else. Giving is contagious, even when the gift is time.

Walk with Generous People

Growing up, my parents always told me, "Rachel, you become who you hang out with." When I was in high school, I thought they were just telling me not to hang out with sketchy teenagers. Now that I've gotten some perspective, I think what they really meant was that I should spend my time with people I want to be like. If you want to be generous and kind, then spend time with generous and kind people. If you want to be selfish, then hang out with selfish people.

Personally, I want to hang out with people who are generous with their time and attention—and I want to avoid people who aren't. When Winston and I first moved back to Nashville, we went out to eat with a couple who seemed like people we would get along with. However, they would not stop talking about themselves the entire time. Winston and I combined didn't say more than three words. The experience was completely exhausting, and it didn't take us long before we knew we weren't going to click with this couple. I felt like I needed a social detox when we got home.

You always remember the people in your life who care about you, celebrate with you, and comfort you. Invest your time in people like this. More importantly, strive to be that type of person yourself.

A GENEROUS LIFE

Dream for a second. Think about all the giving you could do with your money if you were debt-free! How many people could you help if you didn't have a car payment and student loan payment? That may seem like a long way off, but this is where financial responsibility and behavior combine to create a powerful force of change in your life and in the world around you.

So many people think good financial management begins and ends with balance sheets and investment accounts. Those are important, but it's what good money habits *allow you to do* that matters the most. And I believe that the most important thing you can do with your money—and the most fun you can have with money—is to give it. Plus, when you manage money well, get out of debt, and build wealth, you end up with something even more valuable than money. You get time. You get options. You get to choose where to invest your energy and how to live out your passions because you aren't worried about making ends meet. When you combine time, money, options, passion, and a habit of giving, you can literally change the world!

16

What Now?

Hearing my phone alarm go off at 5:00 a.m. is still hard sometimes. At the start of this book, I told you that getting up early is a new habit I have in my life. Some days it's easier than others to get my feet on the floor. But the weirdest thing happened. After a few weeks of my new morning routine, I started waking up around 5:00 a.m. even if my alarm wasn't set. Like on a Saturday. When I actually *wanted* to sleep. Sure, I can roll over and go back to sleep, but I still wake up. My body just knows when it's time to get up.

That's the great thing about habits. They become automatic. The consistent choices you make with your money from this point on will dictate if you have healthy money habits or destructive ones. I may not always enjoy getting up at 5:00 a.m., but it has become routine. Like budgeting, it's not something I necessarily look forward to, but if I don't do it, things feel out of control.

The seven money habits we've discussed throughout this book are like that too. Some habits will be easier than others. Sometimes you won't want to do one. Sometimes it'll seem easier to make a big impulse purchase, swipe a credit card, or not talk to your spouse about money. But, the longer you practice these habits, the more automatic they'll become. And, when you try to go one way when your new healthy habits are telling you to go another, you'll know something's off.

The exciting thing is, wherever you are in this journey, something is different today than it was when you first picked up this book. You know some things now that maybe you didn't know before. You've had to face some things that maybe you didn't want to face. You've had to take an honest look at your life, your goals, and your money—maybe for the first time. You've had to think about what you value, what is really important to you and your family. You've had to start prioritizing the things you want to do, realizing that in order to do *this*, you probably can't do *that*.

The truth is, you've learned some new things, and that new information may change everything. In the legal world they call it "unringing the bell." Once the bell sounds, you can't unring it. It's happened and you can't deny it. You have to deal with it. When it comes to the seven money habits we've discussed here, you have to decide for yourself if you want to apply these principles and work toward a life you love, or if you're going to dismiss what we've discussed and go back to doing things the way you've always done them, like impulse buying, credit card swiping, and comparison living.

I believe anyone—yes, that means you—can take control of their money and let it work for them to live the life they've always wanted. No, it may not (and probably will not) happen overnight. And, no, you may not be able to have *everything* you want, especially all at once. But little by little, one decision at a time, you can change the direction of your life. You can be more satisfied, more excited, about the life you're living, and you can stop worrying so much about what everyone else seems to have. And, ultimately, in time, you can learn how to love *your* life, not theirs.

Notes

Introduction

1. Charles Duhigg, *The Power of Habit: Why We Do What We Do in Life and Business* (New York: Random House, 2012), 20.

Chapter Four

1. Taylor Tepper, "Americans Are Sinking Further Into Credit Card Debt," *Money Magazine*, December 9, 2015, http://time .com/money/4138675/americans-credit-card-debt-nerdwallet/.
2. Jeffrey Sparshott, "Congratulations, Class of 2015. You're the Most Indebted Ever (For Now)," *The Wall Street Journal*, May 8, 2015, http://blogs.wsj.com/economics/2015/05/08 /congratulations-class-of-2015-youre-the-most-indebted -ever-for-now/.
3. Marine Cole, "Here's Why Our Auto Loan Debt Has Hit $886 Billion," *The Fiscal Times*, March 16, 2015, http://www.thefiscaltimes.com/2015/03/16 /Here-s-Why-Our-Auto-Loan-Debt-Has-Hit-886-Billion.
4. Katie McFadden, "Large Number of Flyers Never Redeem Air Miles Due to Restrictive Terms," Travelers Today, June 3, 2013, http://www.travelerstoday.com/articles/6478/20130603/large -number-flyers-never-redeem-air-miles-due-restrictive-terms.htm.

5. Erin El Issa, "2015 American Household Credit Card Debt Study," NerdWallet, accessed December 15, 2015, http://www.nerdwallet.com/blog/credit-card-data/ average-credit-card-debt-household/.

6. "Using Your Visa Debit Card," Visa, accessed December 15, 2015, https://usa.visa.com/support/consumer/debit-cards.html.

7. "Brain Scans Predict When People Will Buy Products," *ScienceDaily*, Carnegie Mellon University, January 4, 2007, https://www.sciencedaily.com /releases/2007/01/070103201418.htm.

8. Richard Fry, "Young Adults, Student Debt and Economic Well-Being," Pew Research Center, May 14, 2014, http://www.pewsocialtrends.org/2014/05/14 /young-adults-student-debt-and-economic-well-being/.

9. Jay MacDonald, "Dealing with deadbeat friends or family members," Bankrate, May 26, 2006, Accessed October 15, 2015, http://www.bankrate.com/brm/news/pf/20060519a3.asp.

Chapter Eight

1. Ellie Delano, "Arguing About Money May Predict Divorce," *Woman's Day*, July 22, 2013, http://www .womansday.com/relationships/dating-marriage/a48024 /arguing-about-money-predicts-divorce/.

2. Dr. David Stoop and Dr. Jan Stoop, *The Complete Marriage Book: Collected Wisdom from Leading Marriage Experts* (Revell, 2002).

Chapter Ten

1. "Gap Between New and Used Vehicle Payments Widens to Reach an All-Time High," Experian, August 27, 2015, https:// www.experianplc.com/media/news/2015/q2-2015-safm-pt-2/.

2. Nanci Hellmich, "A third of people have nothing saved for

retirement," *USA Today*, August 18, 2014, http://www
.usatoday.com/story/money/personalfinance/2014/08/18
/zero-retirement-savings/14070167/.

3. Jeffrey Sparshott, "Congratulations, Class of 2015. You're
the Most Indebted Ever (For Now)," *The Wall Street Journal*,
May 8, 2015, http://blogs.wsj.com/economics/2015/05/08
/congratulations-class-of-2015-youre-the-most-indebted
-ever-for-now/.

4. Melanie Hicken, "Average wedding bill in 2012: $28,400,"
CNN Money, March 10, 2013, http://money.cnn
.com/2013/03/10/pf/wedding-cost/.

Chapter Eleven

1. Daren Blomquist, "All-Cash Share of U.S. Home
Purchases in May Drops to Lowest Level Since
November 2009," RealtyTrac, July 1, 2015, http://
www.realtytrac.com/news/foreclosure-trends
/may-2015-u-s-home-foreclosure-sales-report/.

Chapter Fourteen

1. Hannah and Kevin Salwen, *The Power of Half: One Family's
Decision to Stop Taking and Start Giving Back* (Mariner
Books, 2011).

PRAISE FOR
LOVE YOUR LIFE, NOT THEIRS

I've never read a book about money that takes this approach—and that's a good thing! Comparison has a way of weaving itself throughout all aspects of our lives, including our money. In *Love Your Life, Not Theirs*, Rachel Cruze outlines the seven money habits that really matter—and they have nothing to do with keeping up with the Joneses!

Candace Cameron-Bure
Actress, author, and co-host of *The View*

Love Your Life, Not Theirs is full of the kind of practical, straightforward advice we've come to expect from Rachel Cruze. She offers guidance on paying down debt, smart saving, and the right way to talk to your spouse about money. These indispensable tips can help with day-to-day spending decisions and put you on a path to establishing healthy financial habits.

Susan Spencer
Editor-in-Chief for *Woman's Day*

Cruze's self-deprecating and honest voice is a great resource for anyone wanting to take charge of their money. With humor and approachability, she helps her readers set themselves up for success and happiness, no matter what current financial state they may be in.

Kimberly Williams-Paisley
New York Times best-selling author of
Where the Light Gets In

In today's world of social media, the temptation to play the comparison game is stronger than ever. *Love Your Life, Not Theirs* is the perfect reminder that, when it comes to money, comparison is a game you can't win. A terrific—and much needed—read.

Jean Chatzky
Financial Editor, NBC TODAY and
Host of HerMoney with Jean Chatzky Podcast

Your thinking has been bullied way too long by the stings of comparison and the strains of debt. *Love Your Life, Not Theirs* is the resource that will show you how to break free from the chains of an unrealistic lifestyle. I love how Rachel gives us practical yet powerful money habits that can be implemented in any situation. You still have the opportunity to create the beautiful life you want financially—this book will show you how!

Lysa TerKeurst
New York Times **best**-selling author and
president of Proverbs 31 Ministries

Comparison robs us of joy, contentment, and gratitude. Thankfully Rachel Cruze shows us how to crush the curse of comparisons in her brilliant and must-read book, *Love Your Life, Not Theirs*. Rachel explains seven simple habits to recalibrate how you see your finances and, ultimately, yourself. Read this book with an open heart to start living the life you really want.

Craig Groeschel
Pastor of Life.Church and *New York Times*
best-selling author of *#Struggles: Following Jesus
in a Selfie-Centered World*

The subtitle is no lie. Rachel Cruze articulately outlines seven money habits that—if you really embrace them—will allow you to live the life you want. *Love Your Life, Not Theirs* is a must-have book if you want to take control of your money once and for all.

Christine Caine
Founder, A21 Campaign

In *Love Your Life, Not Theirs*, Rachel Cruze elucidates one of the biggest traps into which each of us falls: competing with those around us in order to feel happy and valued. She beautifully articulates how to change destructive spending habits, enjoy our lives, and achieve real freedom. This book is a real winner!

Meg Meeker, M.D.
Author of the best seller *Strong Fathers, Strong
Daughters: Ten Secrets Every Father Should Know*

Spoiler Alert—the Joneses are broke! In *Love Your Life, Not Theirs*, Rachel Cruze reinforces the healthy money habits that will allow you to live a life the Joneses only dream of!

Shay and Colette Carl

A verse in Scripture that impacted me deeply and one that I often share is 2 Corinthians 10:12, which says, "When they measure themselves by themselves and compare themselves with themselves, they are without understanding" (NASB). For me, when I pastored a church, would I let the larger size of another man's church bother me, causing me to conclude I was less important? Would I measure my worth based on the greater number of people who attended his church? Peter had this comparison problem with John, and Jesus said to him, "What is that to you? You follow Me!" I had to focus on my own life and not measure my worth based on my comparison with another. The same applies to a mother who watches another mother who seems to do everything right, or a husband who learns of a peer who just purchased a second home in the mountains. These comparisons can put us on a roller-coaster ride of negative emotions, as Rachel Cruze profoundly addresses in *Love Your Life, Not Theirs*. Each of us must learn to love the life God has given us. Otherwise we will make decisions—especially financial ones—to keep up with the Joneses.

Emerson Eggerichs, PhD
President of Love and Respect Ministries and
author of *Mother and Son: The Respect Effect*

Money problems are the fruit of deeper issues. Rachel helps us deal not just with the fruit, but also with the root of financial mismanagement. She distills complex questions into understandable steps. Great book!

Max Lucado
Best-selling author of *Before Amen: The Power of Simple Prayer*

If you want to shake the comparison game and start building the life that you want, *Love your Life, Not Theirs* will be a kind and competent companion on that journey!

Ellie Holcomb
Singer-songwriter

Practical, actionable, personable, and inspiring, Rachel Cruze balances the perfect blend of tough love and encouragement. A money guide for the modern age, *Love Your Life, Not Theirs* is a book every Millennial needs to read.

Ruth Soukup
New York Times best-selling author of *Living Well, Spending Less* and *Unstuffed*

Raise Money-Smart Kids in a Debt-Filled World.

In the #1 *New York Times* bestselling book, *Smart Money Smart Kids*, financial expert and bestselling author Dave Ramsey and his daughter Rachel Cruze equip parents to teach their children how to win with money.

SmartMoneySmartKids.com